Systems: from science to practice

JOHANNES KEPLER
UNIVERSITÄT LINZ

n

Seminarhotel St. Magdalena, Linz

Gary S. Metcalf

Mary C. Edson

Gerhard . Chroust

(eds.)

Systems: from Science to Practice

Proceedings of the

of the Nineteenth IFSR Conversation 2018

April 8 – 13, 2018

St. Magdalena, Linz, Austria

Bibliografische Information der Deutschen Nationalbibliothek:
Die Deutsche Nationalbibliothek verzeichnet diese Publikation in der
Deutschen Nationalbibliografie; detaillierte bibliografische Daten sind im
Internet über http://dnb.dnb.de abrufbar.

The Conversation took place April 8-13, 2018
in St. Magdalena, Linz, Austria

Herstellung und Verlag:
BoD – Books on Demand, Norderstedt, Deutschland
ISBN: 978-3-7481-26454

Welcome to the Proceedings of the IFSR Conversation 2018

Dear Readers!

This volume, the Proceedings, of the IFSR Conversation 2018 in St. Magdalena, Linz Austria, provides in Part I part a historical view of the evolution and growths of Conversations in general from 1980 to 2018. This includes personal views of Gordon Dyer, Alexander Laszlo and Gerhard Chroust. In Part II we present the team reports of the four 4 teams at the Conversation.

Conversations were introduced by Bela H. Banathy at around 1980 as an alternative to the classical conferences. They were in response to the insight that the greatest benefit for participants of a meeting were due to the discussions and conversations between participants and not so much as a result of the formal presentations of papers. Bela's philosophical understanding of complex adaptive social systems as self-organizing entities, that promoted inquiry and innovation (Byrne, 1998; Jenlink & Banathy, 2008) compelled him define and establish conversations as a face-to-face meetings (without formal presentation!) where the teams discuss in a self-guided way topics of scientific and social importance (Dyer 2016a , Dyer 2016b, Dyer 2018).

The first Conversation took place in 1982 in a small, cozy inn ('Pension Seewinkel') in Fuschl-am-See on the shore of Lake Fuschl, near Salzburg. The success encouraged the IFSR to convene a Conversation every second year (see Lazslo, 2019, Chroust 2019b for details) with generous subsidies from the IFSR. Additional Conversations of the 'Fuschl type' have been organized in many locations around the world: (Laszlo, 2019) . Increased demands on the accessibility and professional infrastructure of the location made it necessary to move the IFSR Conversations to Kloster Pernegg (a former monastery from the 15th century) in 2010 and for the last four conversations (2012 to2018) to the St. Magdalena seminar hotel on the outskirts of Linz, Austria. A novelty of the 2018 Conversation was that we had to get along without a subsidy from the IFSR, and thus charge the full costs to the participants .

In the IFSR Conversations traditionally three to six of four to eight members meet for five days to develop conceptual models and intensify their understanding of their team's topic. They are free to modify their topic. After the end of the Conversation the teams document their findings at first in a short report which is published in the IFSR Newsletter (Chroust, 2018) . A more comprehensive report in proceedings of the Conversation.

According to tradition the 2018 IFSR Conversation was announced with a 'Call for Topics' to a broad scientific systems audience. In November 2017 there were nine considered for participation in the 2018 Conversation. After intensive discussions of the Executive Committee of the IFSR, five topics were selected. One unfortunately finally could not participate due to time constraints of the participants, which left four teams to meet at St. Magdalena with the following topics:

1. Systems Practice – team leaders: Nam Nguyen and Constantin Malik

2. What is Systems Science? - team leaders: Gary Smith and Jennifer Makar

3. Active and Healthy Aging – team leaders: Shankar Sankaran and Gerhard Chroust and

4. Data Driven Systems Engineering Approaches – team leader : Ed Carroll

All four teams worked very engaged and dedicated, only interrupted by Wednesday (April 11) afternoon when we took off from work and went to downtown Linz. We visited the Ars Electronica Museum, which calls itself the "Museum of the ('digital') future" and offers exhibits and hands-on experimentation specifically demonstrating the technological developments and their impact on society, art, and people.

On Friday morning each team gave a short presentation to all other participants.

After the Conversation short team reports of their findings were published in the October issue of the Newsletter IFSR, vol 35, no 1 (Chroust, 2018). The details and and the comprehensive reports are collected in this proceedings volume (Metcalf, 2019).

Looking back at the 2018 Conversation we believe that again we had made considerable progress in the chosen topics. We want to thank all participants and especially the team leaders for their enthusiasm, work, and effort.

The proceedings are an impressive addition to the past proceedings of the IFSR Conversations (see section "Fuschl/IFSR Conversations, 1982 – 2018 " later in this book).

Mary C. Edson   *Gary S. Metcalf*   *Gerhard Chroust*

References:

Byrne, D. S. (1998). Complexity theory and the social sciences : an introduction. Routledge 1998.

Chroust, G. (editor) (2018) , FSR Newsletter vol 35, No 1 (October 2018) International Federation for Systems Research}, 32pp.

Chroust G. (2019). : 25 YEARS OF IFSR CONVERSATIONS – LOOKING BACK . In: Metcalf, G,S, Edson, M.C. and and Chroust, G. , Systems: from Science to Practice Proceedings of the Nineteenth IFSR Conversation 2018, April 2019, pp. 14-16

Dyer, G. (2016a). Guidebook for designing and sustaining effective conversation.

http://www.ifsr.org/wp-content/uploads/2016/02/guide-effective-conversation_V8_DEC16.pdf

Dyer, G. (2016b). Guidebook for designing and sustaining effective conversation   addendum for team   leaders   http://www.ifsr.org/wp-content/uploads/2016/02/guide-effective-conversation-TEAMLEADERS_V6_DEC16.pdf

Dyer, G (2018) Evolution: Unfit for Purpose - A pathway towards a better future, Milton Contact , Cambridge, UK, 2018, 978-1-911526-26-1 ,pp. 169

Laszlo, A. (2019). Brief Background on the Fuschl/IFSR Conversations. In: Metcalf, G.S, Edson, M.C. and Chroust, G. , Systems: from Science to Practice - Proceedings of the Nineteenth IFSR Conversation 2018, Books on Demand, Norderstedt, Germany, 2019, ISBN 978-3-7481-26454 *(this book)*

Metcalf G.S. (2019) : Gary S. Metcalf, G.S. and Edson, M.C. and Chroust, G. (eds.) : Systems: from Science to Practice - Proceedings of the 19th IFSR Conversation 2018}, {BoD - Books on Demand, Norderstedt, Germany}, ISBN 978-3-7481-26454 pp. 144

Previous Proceedings can be found on http://www.ifsr.org/index.php/publications/conversations/

Part I : IFSR Conversation 2018 – Looking Back

Personal Perspectives on Conversations – Past, Present and Future
Gordon Dyer

Bela Banathy Centenary

As we enter 2019 it is appropriate to remember this year as the centenary of the birth of Bela Banathy (1919 - 2003) [1]who founded the Conversation movement almost 40 years ago. One testimony to Bela's contribution to the systems field is that the biennial Fuschl Conversations (since 2008 called the IFSR Conversations) still continue and remain a highlight in the programme of the International Federation for Systems Research.

Wikipedia carries his detailed biography from birth in Hungary on 1 December 1919, his service and torrid time in the national army during and immediately post-World War II, eventual emigration to the USA in 1951 and his emergence as an outstanding linguist, educator, systems scientist and author. However, the biography is simply factual and apart from implying huge stoicism, determination and intelligence gives little indication of his ability to influence and stimulate new thinking and change in others.

How did this quietly spoken and sometimes-self-effacing man become so charismatic? Those who knew him will have their own answer to that question. I can only share my personal views having first met him at the 1987 ISGSR Conference in Budapest. There is no doubt that his warmth of welcome and an open smile was important giving the impression when we spoke, what I was saying was worth his time listening. But my key reflections are based around what he said, and how he conveyed his message to his audience - fundamentally through metaphors which he intuitively knew would both appeal and challenge. In short, it was impossible to let them go out of your mind. Examples of this kind of messages were:

"If systems thinking is all that it is cracked up to be why can't we use it to help with some of the major issues in the world?"

"Don't ask me how to do it. You are all supposed to be creative human beings. You must solve problems of the future in your own context. You must design your own future."

The Grandchild's Question and his response

But the most powerful influence on me was his "grandchild 's question" which I first heard him present at the 1991 Asilomar conversation. He introduced this through a hypothetical scenario which he said would be his nightmare and source of personal shame if it were ever to happen. His grandson was sitting on his knee and they were watching TV together. This pleasantness was changed by a switch to the latest TV news programme showing a dreadful scene of man's inhumanity in some part of the world. His grandson then turned to him and asked:

"Grandad, you are old, you are supposed to be wise, what have you done about this? What kind of a world are you leaving for me?"

That scenario has never left my mind.

Bela went on to produce many important publications in response to the hypothetical question, arguing that we need to become conscious of how homo sapiens sapiens had evolved in a way which was sustainable with the environment for many 1000s of years. With such "evolutionary consciousness" we should then "evolve consciously" in terms of the characteristics of future social systems that we allowed to develop or evolve, i.e. we should design our future not just let the future happen. His first contribution was to suggest a framework for an evolutionary guidance system, in that social systems and their sub-systems would consciously evolve towards a vision of where advances in technology is not the main driver but takes into account other crucial human domains. In this he included social justice, economic justice, a scientific dimension based on ethical science, technology which is aimed at conflict resolution and not warfare, quality of life for all, genuine participation in choice. This vision of designing the future was accompanied within a set of clearly defined ethics, including: "all those affected by a future system should have the right to be involved in its design, no one should have systems designed or imposed on them". This in turn implied that those traditionally considered to be part of the environment and therefore outside of consideration should now be included in the design process. Also, as time passed and new members joined the system, the process of design would need to be on-going and dynamic. He brought all his ideas together in the classic "Designing Social systems in a Changing World" [2] which also contained the controversial idea that a new competence in social systems design was essential to empower people to direct their progress and create a truly participative democracy.

Conversation and Social System Design

His other fundamental suggestion was that any discussions aimed at "social system design" should be carried out using a different style of dialogue. This is what he, and we now, call "conversation" and is still generally adopted as basis for most of the topics of the biennial Fuschl/IFSR Conversation events at Linz. The activity assumes a free-wheeling, consensus-seeking style of discussion. This is the exact opposite to the aim of debate, where the outcome sought is basically "I win - you lose". This is the normal process of politics, the law and typically academia. Bela strongly argued that the ambition of social system design required a process of aiming for "win-win". The early IFSR and ISI[1] conversations were largely focussed in exploring conversation itself, often with trigger questions relating to the kind of education system that would be required to bring about the new competencies for social system design and what has come to be known as evolutionary learning.

The IFSR and ISI events [3] carried out over the 20 years from 1982 enabled us to learn a great deal about the issues surrounding conversation and the factors which can lead to their success or failure in practice. This led to the publication of a two Volume Compendium of contributions (2005 [4] , 2008 [5]) from IFSR colleagues and the continuation of conversation at Fuschl and Linz. However, little progress was made in the area of application of the systems design in education which Bela had dreamed of, and no real traction had been made with the application of "social system design" to the outside world. There are a number of reasons for this:

* The education field is currently limited to maintenance learning and dominated by politics. For example, in the UK no impact is detectable, not least because the education system has become a political debating zone and where powerful teaching unions resist change. The essence of argument is around standards. Any changes take place on the basis of tinkering with curriculum rather than on the kind of fundamental shift that Banathy called for.

* There was scepticism indeed from some, antagonism, towards the concept of designing the mid- to longer-term future of social systems. This was mostly from those with the world view that systems thinking and practice related only to "feasible and desirable" change within existing systems, or to immediate replacement systems.

* Also, the idea that conversation between team members would continue in-between IFSR conversations did not materialise for two reasons. Firstly, once back in one's normal environment, day-job pressures typically restricted this from happening. Second, turnover within teams from conversation to conversation, a requirement of IFSR policy to more widely share the benefit of their financial support, made this impractical.

---

[1] The ISI (International Systems Institute) was created by Bela Banathy in order to support conversation events.

" The death of Bela in 2003, and the loss of his inspiring leadership was the end of social system design as a dominant theme for IFSR conversations. This ending was especially unfortunate for Gordon Rowland and myself as we had begun, through the "Y3K conversations" as part of the Conversations in 2000 and 2002, to consider markers for the vision of a distant future. Y3K (the year 3000) was not a precise target. It was a metaphor for a longer-term future and was a deliberate attempt to forestall any comments of the form "It can't be done." Anything might happen in a distant future. The choice still remains to us. We do have options over first steps we might suggest individually and collectively to adjust our view of systems thinking and change pathways towards the future.

Communicating the case for change

New topics emerged as the norm for IFSR conversations from 2004 to replace social system design. This also reflected a desire within the IFSR to focus on what were seen as current pressing issues, and in a period of time when funds are limited, to show practical outcomes from the expense of the Fuschl/IFSR Conversation. This reflect a return to the "feasible and desirable" for systems action. I have some sympathy with this strategy given that some recent topics have focussed on transfer of conversation practice into the wider community, and design of formal systems education programmes.

However, our World of 2019 is a very much more worrying place than one which was evident to Bela Banathy and the other leaders of the national and international systems societies who met at the first Fuschl conversation in 1982. Yet the interest and efforts of the systems community as a whole, and the IFSR activity which is a leading part of it, remains focussed on theoretical, scientific and technical aspects of systems modelling. The papers I attempt to read in our Journals are often highly complex in nature and often contain an indulgence in new words which reduce communication internally and prevent understanding externally. Yet effective communication should be at the centre of our objectives. We need to ensure that the reports on Conversation do not have the same indulgence. They are distributed to a wide audience, and potentially are our best communication channel to the outside world and must be understandable.

The systems community needs to adjust the balance between investigating activities and publishing reports on scientific/technical topics, and those on knowledge transfer. The transfer strategy itself needs to be modified, with any developments of formal qualifications to be complemented by introducing a much simpler level of systems ideas to a broader spectrum of the population. This would lead to more people gaining a better understanding of the possibility of counterintuitive outcomes and influence deeper consideration in making future decisions and acting on them. Influencing a larger section of the general population will provide a faster route to improved prospects for a better and sustainable future, than by simply educating a minority. This is not to understate the resistance of adults to change. This implies careful targeting within the population, to those with most potential to gain lay understanding of systems thinking and with leadership experience, or the capacity to assume it. It also requires presentation of a convincing case capable of nudging their perception and encouraging action for change.

Systems Community Values

Over recent years the systems community has debated whether its activity is a "science". This is understandable given that science is typically funded more favourably by national governments.

I am reminded of a classic question posed to students of the History and Philosophy of Science, i.e. "Is science value free?". The answer is "no", the justification coming from the evidence that what we understand today as science, is derived from the areas of the physical and natural world mankind has mainly chosen to explore in the past and that was determined by the contemporary value system. One is pointed to the synthesis of mauveine (mauve dye) in 1856 by William Perkins. This led to its mass production along with the demise of the madder plant growing industry, the previous source of mauve dye. This was followed by an expansion in chemistry research with an emphasis placed on dyes, explosives and gases. By comparison there was little scientific interest in other areas at that time, e.g. human factors and health. People, the workers, were regarded as disposable "units". This area only came to be considered as "appropriate science" in the 20th century. The value system of the 19th century was very much based on need for competition, to gain manufacturing advantage, national status and overseas possessions. This meant that areas of chemistry and physics which increased national potential for war were largely pursued.

So, I ask myself an analogous question. "Is systems science value free?" The historians of the future will give the same answer, "no". What will determine their understanding of systems science at that future time, will be determined by the choices we make now. Given the sustainability issues facing humanity and the desperate inequalities and inequities that exist, to reject the idea that systems practice can have value in the creation of a better future, and is limited in application to the "here and now" seems a derogation of duty. It also reminds me of the old English proverb about Emperor Nero who "fiddled while Rome burned".

We can still do something

I will now return to my personal response to Bela's proposals for social system design. Initially, I was overwhelmed by the concept and ethical stance within it. These ideas were beyond my understanding of systems thinking, and problems viewed at world-systems level seemed insurmountable. However, as stated above, the grandchild's question stubbornly refused to leave my mind. When I first heard the question, I too was old. Well, I was approaching 60. I had done nothing. I felt somewhat ashamed, but I could find plenty of excuses for my lack of action.

However, with increasing experience of conversation within IFSR/ISI teams and also with small external groups, I came to see it was possible to provide guidance for action within a small social or work group. My target is a systems-lay individual, with some leadership experience and perhaps concerns with current behaviour patterns in their group. If many such "small fires" can be started in this way, then this might trigger change in the larger social systems which contains these smaller groups. So, in a new book [6], I

"   encourage the reader to reflect on and to challenge their world view. I do this through presenting my own experiences and journey of change - from being entirely focused on the benefits of technology, then exposure to systems ideas, and then to wider systems experience and "conversation".

"   introduce and demonstrate, en-route, basic systems thinking in a way which those unfamiliar can easily appreciate and use themselves. These are the necessary and sufficient concepts of emergence, counterintuitive outcomes, synergy and interdependence. They apply to all social systems, including small groups.

"   demonstrate a flexible methodology which allows a small group to move towards a better vision of their future. The methodology is dynamic, highly adaptable to the reader's own context and assumes on-going iteration and review. Case studies, including use within a small primary school where staff had been through a period of trauma and needed help in finding a way forward, are described.

"   then provide guidance on how the reader can do this for a small social or work group they are involved with, with conversation - aimed at sustaining creative synergy - at its core.

So, from my perspective social system design as a concept is not totally dead, but is adaptable to a small group case. Clearly, this is but one approach to one target set, but it is a start to build on.

Gordon Rowland and Doug Walton have suggested that the ISI conversation group might be reconvened for a conversation in the USA to celebrate Bela Banathy's centenary. The emails which have circulated as a result between ex-ISI members have confirmed that Bela has been a great influence in their lives too. It would be wonderful to share their reports on these influences if such a conversation can be arranged.

Some proposals

Drawing on Bela's grandson's scenario, IFSR is a key source of "systems wisdom". In a future world which continues to deteriorate, would not the recently born, and yet to be born children, be entitled to say - "What did the IFSR do about it?"

I urge the IFSR to reconsider the value system which defines its strategies. This should be carried out through a conversation style of dialogue within its governance structure, and then carried forward with members in the biennial IFSR Conversations, beginning with 2020.

This challenge could provide the basis of the overall theme, and the trigger question for the 2020 Conversation, say:

What value system should IFSR project and to what audience?

From this a number of possible team sub-topics could emerge, e.g.:

1.   What should be the balance of IFSR interest and concern between the "here and now" and "the future" for systems application?

2.   Could the IFSR better communicate its findings and applications based on its values?.

3.   What role might IFSR play in encouraging national and international societies to promote systems thinking with a systems-lay leadership population? Who should be the target leadership sets? Should space be allocated in the Journal of Systems Research and Behavioral Science. for publishing Research papers in this field?

4.   What are the key systems concepts which need to be conveyed to a systems-lay leadership population, and what suitable vehicles could be used for this, e.g. MOOCs, DVDs, podcasts, printed learning materials?

The programme could still allow for one or more pressing technical questions to be included.

A final personal note. Since 1991 I have had the good fortune to participate in some 16   ISI, Fuschl and IFSR Conversations held in Asilomar, Fuschl, Pernegg and Linz. This has covered all the various roles as team member, team leader, and co-convenor. I have gained enormously in understanding and insight as a result and the experience has been the key stimulus to my subsequent publications and actions. En route, I have made some great and lasting friends as a result. I sincerely hope that current and future systems thinkers will have access to similar opportunities.

I invite all members of IFSR to encourage the Federation to continue organising a biennial Conversation. Also, whether members represent national or international societies, they themselves incorporate the conversation method for collective dialogue in at least part of their own programmes.

I end by wishing the IFSR increasing success in acting in the future as the focus of global systems activity, and similarly to the IFSR Conversations in being an exemplar for its practice and guidance.

[1] https://en.wikipedia.org/wiki/Bela H. Banathy (accessed 27 December 2018)

[2] Banathy, B. H. Designing Social Systems in a Changing World, (1996), Plenum NY

[3] Lazlo, A. A brief Background on the Fuschl Conversations, (2013), IFSR Newsletter vol. 30, No. 1, pp. 6-8

[4] Jenlink.P.M. with Banathy.B.H., (eds) Dialogue as a Means of Collective Conversation, (2005), Kluwer Academic/Plenum, NY

[5] Jenlink.P.M. with Banathy.B.H., (eds) Dialogue as a Collective Means of Design Conversation, (2008), Springer, NY

[6] Dyer.G.C, Evolution - Unfit for Purpose - a pathways towards a better future. (2018), Milton Contact, Cambridge, UK (www.miltoncontact.co.uk accessed 27 December 2018)

Chroust Janie, 2009: Lake Fuschl

A Brief Background of the Fuschl Conversations
Alexander Laszlo

(This is an updated version of A. Laszlo's paper in the IFSR Newsletter, Vol. 30, No. 1, 2013. Pp. 6-8)

Alexander Laszlo is President of the Bertalanffy Center for the Study of Systems Science (BCSSS)

What came to be known as the "Fuschl Conversations" took place every two years at Fuschl-am-See in Austria near Salzburg from 1982 through 2008. They comprised the more international component of a series of Conversation Events that included a parallel set of conversations that took place on a yearly basis in Pacific Grove, California, favoring Northern American participation from 1990 through 2006. Respectively, these conversation events became known as the Fuschl Conversations (biennially) and the Asilmor Conversations (annually). By 2010, the Fuschl Conversations were continued under the name of the IFSR Conversations in Pernegg (Northern Austria) and from 2012 onward as the IFSR Conversations in Linz, Austria.

Originally, this series of conversation events known as "the Conversations on the Comprehensive Redesign of Educational Systems" but the name was later changed and broadened to "the Conversations on the Comprehensive Redesign of Societal Systems" to better reflect the systemic recognition that educational systems cannot be redesigned separately from the rest of the societal systems with which they are intertwingled. In their book on *Dialogue as a Collective Means of Design Conversation* (2007), editors Patrick Jenlink and Bela Banathy provide a brief history of the Conversation Movement.

THE FUSCHL SYMPOSIUM '82

"The first conversation took place at the Fuschl Lake in Austria in April 1982. A group of systems scholars met in a small hotel at the Fuschl Lake, near Salzburg. Participants came from three continents, representing ten cultures. They were invited as leaders of various systems societies. The conversation was organized by the International Systems Institute. The group spent five days in two conversation teams, addressing the question: How can we apply the insights gained from systems thinking and systems practice to promote human betterment and to improve the human condition? By the end of the conversations, the teams defined eighty items to guide the work of the various systems societies and become an agenda for the conversations that follow. Following the Fuschl Conversation, a group of us – officers of the International Federation of Systems Research (IFSR) – attended the Board Meeting of the IFSR, where the Board decided to provide funding for Fuschl Conversations." (Banathy 2008, p. 25)

The preceding paragraph was taken from Banathy's chapter titled "The Conversation Movement", on pages 25-38. As described by him, given the success of the first five Fuschl Conversation events and the initial Asilomar Conversation, he decided to establish the International Systems Institute (ISI) in 1992 as an umbrella organization under which the Conversation Events could be nurtured and developed. It was Banathy's hope that an official organizational identity would help scholars and academic colleagues – considered Research Fellows of the Institute – to obtain funding and support from their respective institutions for attendance at the Conversation Events.

The ISI was set up as a complementary vehicle to the older and larger International Society for the Systems Sciences (ISSS) to carry out the special purpose of serving as a vehicle for conversation-based inquiry in the systems sciences – an approach not actively fostered by the ISSS at the time. The association of systems societies to which both the ISI and the ISSS belong is the International Federation for Systems Research (IFSR - http://www.ifsr.org/index.php/member-societies/). The IFSR came into existence 26 years after the founding of the ISSS and 12 years before the ISI. At the European Meeting for Cybernetics and Systems Research (EMCSR) in Vienna in 1976, a proposal was put forward to set up a European Federation for Cybernetics and Systems Research [IFSR Newsletter 1(1), 1981]. These plans were revised and reshaped at the EMCSR meeting in Linz in 1978 with the result that on 12 March 1980, the IFSR was established as a joint initiative of the Netherlands Society for Systems Research (SN), the International Society for General Systems Research (ISGSR), [2] and the Austrian Society for Cybernetic Studies (ASCS) [IFSR Newsletter, 1981. P. 2]. When the ISI was begun in 1982, it did not split off from the ISGSR as some have claimed. In fact, Banathy was President of the ISGSR for the 1984-85 term, which is after he had founded the ISI. While these two organizations developed separately, they were in no way in competition or antagonism with each other. Through the establishment of the ISI, Banathy sought to provide a vehicle for systems thinkers, designers, scholars and practitioners to engage with each other in an interactive and conversational format not then found in the ISGSR. Nevertheless, membership flowed easily through both organizations at the same time.

Bela Banathy also held the Presidency of the IFSR from 1994-1998. Under his lead, the IFSR gradually began taking on the administrative and logistical aspects of the Fuschl Conversations. This made sense from a variety of organizational standpoints given that both the Secretariat of the IFSR, and the Fuschl Conversation events (and all the subsequent conversations that continue its legacy) are located in Austria. In addition, Gerhard Chroust, who served as IFSR's Secretary General for many years, has been a key player in the Fuschl Conversations from the time of Banathy's Presidency of the IFSR through 2008, and in the IFSR Conversations in Pernegg in 2010 and in Linz from 2012 through 2018, as well. Chroust continues to be an important figure in the IFSR, particularly as concerns the organization of what is popularly referred to as the Linz Conversation events every two years. In Banathy's previously cited chapter on "The Conversation Movement", he describes how …

"The various conversations that followed the first Fuschl event, have been organized and coordinated by the International Systems Institute, in cooperation with International Federation of Systems Research, and with several member organizations of the Federation. By now we [the ISI] have held thirty conversations; ten Conversations in Fuschl, Austria; eight regional conversations: two in Crete; one each in England, Finland, Greece, Hungary; and three in Spain. Since 1989, we have held twelve international Conversations at the Asilomar Conference Center in California and established the Asilomar Conversation Community (ACC) as a conversation community of the International Systems Institute." (Banathy 2008: 26)

Although Banathy did not attend the Fuschl Conversations after 1996, he still exercised a strong influence on the shape and scope of the various conversation events. When he passed away in 2003, the ISI effectively ceased to operate as the primary holding container of the Conversation Events, and the IFSR took over all aspects of the sponsorship and running of the Fuschl meetings. This was a natural transition since the IFSR had been providing sponsorship of these events since early on[3]. Nevertheless, numerous other Conversation Events inspired by the Fuschl and Asilomar Conversations of the ISI continue to be held in other parts of the world, such as the Conversaciones del Extremo Sur which former ISSS President Enrique Herrscher began in 2012 in the southern most city of the world, Ushuaia, Argentina, where four successful international Conversation Events have been held since then, and a fifth is planned for 2019.

Banathy always considered conversation as a "future creating disciplined inquiry" (Banathy, 1996, p. 45) when engaged with in the spirit of social systems design (SSD). According to Banathy, two complementary modes of dialogue comprise design conversation: generative dialogue and strategic dialogue (ibid., p. 218, following the work of David Bohm On Dialogue (1996)). One provides a process through which individuals become friends and partners in learning/designing and a community

---

[2] Between 1962 and 1988, the ISSS was known as the ISGSR and subsequently did it become the ISSS.
[3] The proceedings of the Fuschl/IFSR Conversations from 1996 onward can be found on the IFSR website at http://www.ifsr.org/index.php/category/archives/proceedings-of-ifsr-conversations/.

generates common meaning. The other focuses on particular tasks in the creation of solutions for a specific social circumstance. The complementary dynamic between generative and strategic dialogue echoes M. Scott Peck's (1987, p. 104) exhortation: "community-building first, problem-solving second."

I began participating in the Fuschl Conversations in 1988 during the time I earned my Master's degree in the *History and Sociology of Science* from the University of Pennsylvania. Looking back as a historian on the more than thirty-six years of conversations, it appears to me that this modality of "future creating disciplined inquiry" is as relevant and needed to contemporary efforts at individual and collective meaning making as ever it was. Indeed, these are times that call for connective intelligence put to use for collective intelligence put to use for collective creativity so that we, as a species, may more frequently express collective wisdom. It is a time to remember things yet to come, to reflect collectively on our true potential as curators of patterns of thrivability. By engaging in thriving conversations that foster thrivable futures we at once rise up and lift each other up so as to see past individual blind-spots and see through to realizable collective aspirational ideals. This is a time to re-member our world in conversation with ancestors and with those not yet born, and to re-story our collective self through the ubuntu[4] of interbeing. Mary Oliver admonished that we "Pay attention. Be astonished. Tell about it." These, she said, are the instructions for living a life. Together, through the ongoing evolution of conversation content and process, we lend direction, dimension, and meaning to the narratives of our time. In so doing, we create the conditions that are conducive to life by being the systems we wish to see in the world — together.

Recommended Reading and References

Banathy, Bela H. and Patrick M. Jenlink (eds). Dialogue as a Means for Collective Communication. Dordrecht: Kluwer, 2007.

Banathy, Bela H. Designing Social Systems in a Changing World. Plenum, 1996.

Bohm, David. On Dialogue. New York: Routledge, 1996.

François, Charles. International Encyclopedia of Systems and Cybernetics. K. G. Saur, 1997.

Hammond, Debora. The Science of Synthesis: Exploring the Social Implications of General Systems Theory. University Press of Colorado, 2010.

IFSR Newsletter. International Secretariat of the Austrian Society for Cybernetic Studies, Prof. F. de P. Hanika (ed.). Vol. 1, No. 1, Autumn 1981.

The International Systems Institute (ISI) http://www.systemsinstitute.com/about-2 http://www.systemsinstitute.com/about-2/the-isi-story

Jenlink, Patrick and Banathy, Bela H. (eds). Dialogue as a Collective Means of Design Conversation. New York: Springer, 2008.

Laszlo, Alexander. Conversation Communities in Context: A Retrospective Perspective, in the special issue of *Constructivist Foundations* on Composing Conferences: Exploring Alternatives to the Traditional Conference Format, M. Hohl & B. Sweeting (Guest Eds.), Vol. 11, No. 1, 15 November 2015. Pp. 45-56.

Laszlo, Alexander. A brief background on the Fuschl Conversations. In IFSR Newsletter, Vol. 30, No. 1, 2013. Pp. 6-8.Laszlo, Alexander and Krippner, Stanley. Systems Theories: Their origins, foundations, and development. In Jordan, J.S. (ed.) Systems Theories and A Priori Aspects of Perception. Elsevier, 1996.

Laszlo, Alexander and Laszlo, Kathia Castro. The making of a new culture: Learning conversations and design conversations in social evolution. In P.M. Jenlink & B.H. Banathy (Eds.), Dialogue as a Collective Means of Design Conversation. New York: Springer, 2008.

Laszlo, Alexander and Laszlo, Kathia Castro. The evolution of evolutionary systems design. World Futures, 2002, Vol. 58, No. 6-7.

Laszlo, Kathia Castro and Laszlo, Alexander. The conditions for thriving conversations. In B.H. Banathy & P.M. Jenlink (Eds.), Dialogue as a Means for Collective Communication. Dordrecht: Kluwer, 2007.

Oliver, Mary. Excerpt from the poem "Sometimes" in Red Bird. Boston: Beacon Press, 2009, p. 37.

Peck, M. Scott. The Different Drum: Community building and peace. Simon and Schuster, 1987

---

[4] A notion, derived from the belief system of the Xhosa and Zulu peoples of Southern Africa, that expresses the sentiment that "I am because we are", i.e., the essence of my being is conditioned and ultimately defined by the collective interactions of all with whom I come in contact (see Archbishop Desmond Tutu for more at http://www.ghfp.org/Portals/ghfp/documents/Foreword_ArchbishopTutu_final.pdf).

My 25 YEARS OF FUSCHL/IFSR CONVERSATIONS (1994 to 2018)
Gerhard Chroust

LOOKING BACK with pride and nostalgia

In 1992 I commenced in my position as Professor for Systems Engineering and Automation at the Johannes Kepler University Linz and soon after my inauguration, my then Head of Institute, Franz Pichler, asked me to take over the office of the Secretary/Treasurer (later called 'Secretary General') of the IFSR.

He handed over this documentation on this - to me unknown - federation including financial reports. On looking through this I noticed a amount spent on a "Conversation" and - as it seemed – with no sizeable effect or outcome.

The next such Conversation was scheduled for one week in spring 1994 in a small village in Austria. I therefore decided to go and find out more — and to eliminate these unnecessary costs.

This turned out quite otherwise! I arrived in the little village of Fuschl am See, near Salzburg, and made my way to a small inn: Pension Seewinkel. 23 person were present in the restaurant of this pension. Being late and noticing an empty chair, I sat down – oops! A mistake! I was immediately told that this chair was not for me – it was placed there as a symbol for the generations to come, whom we should always keep in mind. I introduced myself as the new Secretary of the IFSR and thus the person with the thick check book .

Fig. 1: Fuschl Conversion 1994

I was welcomed by the leader of the meeting and the current IFSR president, Bela H.Banathy, a soft-spoken, friendly and very impressive personality. I participated in the discussion of the week-long Conversation and was more than impressed. The group was dedicated, dynamic, and full of responsibility for the future – a truly systemic gathering. I very soon realized the value of these conversations. The only change I decided on was to document the outcome of the Conversation for the outside world and to establish a proper organizational structure – administrations not being Bela's strong side. I introduced suitable regulations for participation, attendance and registration of attendees and - most important the publication of proceedings of the Conversation (see ,List of Fuschl/IFSR Conversation Proceedings' in this volume).

Pension Seewinkel was charming, very cozy, and the conversation arrangements were improvised. Our hosts (Mr. and Ms. Ferstl) were very friendly and nice. We could use the whole house, but had no real meeting rooms: I remember that one team always got together on the ,2nd floor landing'. In good weather we sat on the veranda of the inn. But we had almost no technical support: I still remember Yoshi Horiuchi kneeling in front the inn's printer, trying to make it work.

Fortunately the assistants from my institute were able to assist us - especially by bringing the lacking computer equipment, beamer, flip charts, etc. to the conference location. I want to explicitly thank Manfred Beneder, Christian and Susanne Hofer, and Christoph Hoyer for their support.

From 1982 until 1996 Bela was the focal point and leader of the Conversations: traditionally there were 4 or 5 teams and Bela walked from one team to the other, giving advice, linking their findings and issues to one another and thus supporting the communication between the teams. Since we also had rooms in the inn, we spent long evenings talking.

In 1998 Bela had still organized the Conversation, but was finally not able to attend personally, so Sue McCormick and Gordon Dyer took the lead.

Our situation changed when the inn was taken over by a tenant. It lost its traditional touch and in 2002 the arrangement with Pension Seewinkel suddenly broke: The new tenants could not keep the agreed-upon scheduling – and we were homeless. We were, however, lucky to be able to switch to the Hotel Schlick, still in Fuschl. We were warmly received by our new host, Ms. Hertha Idinger. She offered us more convenience, better rooms and an excellent fish cuisine. But soon the need for technology had also reached the Fuschl Conversation: The participants wanted to be connected with the outside world even during the Conversation. In the first year there was just one telephone cell with a land line connection to the outside world – a poor connection to the internet … and one printer for copying documents.

As a result we broke with a tradition. The Fuschl Conversations left Fuschl. They were now called the "IFSR Conversations". In 2010 we stayed in the seminar hotel Kloster Pernegg, Lower Austria, a former monastery. In the following year we found an adequate location in Linz, near my university : St. Magdalena. It offered all the conveniences we needed, 4 to 6 rooms for the teams, all properly equipped with flip charts, blackboards and projectors, and – yes – internet connection.

St. Magdalena provided a beautiful view over Linz. On Wednesdays we took the participants down to the center of the city for sightseeing, shopping and having an informal dinner in the evening.

One long tradition was introduced back in 1994 by John Winchester and his wife and children: Singing. Up to 2016 we devoted one evening to singing: We asked the participants to bring some sheets of music and texts.

Participants from the different countries brought their local music along – and we sang together and had lots of fun. On several occasions Yoshi Horiushi brought a loudspeaker and a tape recorder along, including some magnetic tapes with Japanese songs which we tried to follow in transliterate texts. Once in Hotel Schlick his equipment did not work - so I pulled my car up to the window of the restaurant rooms and played the music on my car's recorder.

In 2005 the generous subsidy of the Austrian Government was stopped. As a consequence we had to reduce the financial support of the IFRSR conversations . In 2018 the participants had to carry all direct costs of the Conversation themselves.

In 2016 we introduced a change in our dissemination policy: we printed the proceedings of the Conversations with a Publisher-on-Demand ('BoD Germany'). The major advantage was that suddenly we had an international distribution channel, both for the hard copy books and (as an additional bonus) for their identical e-book-editions. The only drawback was that we cold not offer the full proceedings on our homepage as free downloads any more.

During these years more than 200 different persons took part in the Conversations – sometimes accompanied by partners, a few times even with their children.

The participants of the Fuschl/IFSR community were fascinating people, full of dedication, responsibility and also scientific experts.

Looking back at the last 25 years, in which we held 13 Conversations we had to accept that running Conversations became more difficult every year: The hectic of our time made it more difficult for participants to take a whole week off, despite St. Magdalena offering sufficiently fast internet connections. The other disadvantage was, that with the phasing out of the EMCSR-conferences the IFSR Conversations became a small event without any parallel larger event. We also moved the IFSR Board Meeting to Linz, adjacent to the Conversations, but there were few persons who were both participants of the Conversation and also members of the IFSR Board.

I personally enjoyed every single Conversation, it was a chance of immersing oneself into complex themes for a whole week. Or, as Charles François once said: "*If you return from Fuschl, to are a different person.*"

Gerhard Chroust

Attemtive Audience, Conversation 2012

Fuschl/IFSR Conversations 1982 – 2018
Status April 2019

The IFSR has published the following proceedings from Fuschl/IFSR-Conversations These proceedings can be found on ifsr.org/publications/conversations/ . Before 1992 , however, the material is incomplete. If you have additional material on the conversations (reports, etc.) please contact Gerhard Chroust (Gerhard.chroust@jku.at).

year	Proceedings	No. of pages
1982	B. H. Banathy. An evolutionary vision of a better future for all - the first F uschl symposium 1982. ifsr.org/publications/conversations/, 1982.	8
1984	Elohim J.L. Are the developing Countries Large Scale Systems Suitable to be tackled by means of the Systems and Cybernetics Approach?. IFSR Newsletter vol No. 9/10 (Autumn-Winter 1984) pp. 7-8.	2
1986	April 1986	?
1988	April 1988	?
1990,	5th Core Conference, April 23-27, 1990	?
1992	G. Dyer. Tenth anniversary fuschl conversation of the internatinal systems science community, report from the systems learning group (incomplete). ifsr.org/publications/conversations/, 1992	21
1994	B.H. Banathy. The Fuschl Story - Fuschl Core-Conversation of the International Systems Science Community (incomplete). ifsr.org/publications/conversations/, 1994	86
1996	B.H. Banathy and G. Chroust, editors. *The Eight Fuschl Conversation (Fuschl, April 14-19,1996).* ÖSGK, Reports of the Austrian Society for Cybernetic Studies, Vienna, September 1996.	53
1998	M. Beneder and G. Chroust, editors. *Designing Social Systems in a Changing World (The Ninth Fuschl Conversation 1998).* ÖSGK, Reports of the Austrian Society for Cybernetic Studies, Vienna, September 1998	82
2000	C. Hofer and G. Chroust, editors. *Social Systems and the Future (The Tenth Fuschl Conversation).* ÖSGK, Reports of the Austrian Society for Cybernetic Studies, Vienna, Nov. 2000	128
2002	C. Hofer and G. Chroust, editors. *The Eleventh Fuschl Conversation).* ÖSGK, Reports of the Austrian Society for Cybernetic Studies, Vienna, Feb. 2003	264
2004	G. Chroust. Fuschl 2004: The 12th fuschl conversation, april 2004. In *Chroust, G., Hofer, C., Hoyer, C. : Proceedings of the Twelfth Fuschl Conversation,* pages 5–6. Inst. f. Systems Engineering and Automation, Johannes Kepler University Linz, Austria, SEA-SR-07, Jan 2005	117
2006	G. Metcalf and G. Chroust. Fuschl 2006 - aims and objectives. In G. Metcalf and G. Chroust, editors, *Pro- ceedings of the Thirteenth Fuschl Conversation, April 22-27, 2006,* pages 6–9. Inst. f. Systems Engineering and Automation, Kepler Univ. Linz, 2006, SEA-SR-13, 2006.	66
2008	G. Chroust, editor. *Proceedings of the Fourteenth Fuschl Conversation, March 29-April 3, 2008.* Inst. f. Systems Engineering and Automation, Johannes Kepler University Linz, Austria, SEA-SR-22, Jan 2009.	48
2010	G. Chroust and G. Metcalf, editors. *Systems for Education, Engineering, Service, and*	80

	Sustainability - Fif- teenth IFSR Conversation. Inst. f. Systems Engineering and Automation, Johannes Kepler University Linz, Austria, SEA-SR-28, August 2010 and [http://ifsr.ocg.at/world/files/$10g$Pernegg-2010-proc.pdf], 2010.	
2012	G. Chroust and G. Metcalf, editors. *Systems and Science at Crossroads - Sixteenth IFSR Conversation.* Inst. f. Systems Engineering and Automation, Johannes Kepler University Linz, Austria, SEA-SR-32, Sept. 2012 and http://www.ifsr.org/wp-content/uploads/2013/04/conversations-2012-magdalena-proc.pdf, 2012	118
2014	M.C. Edson, G.S. Metcalf, G. Chroust, N. Nguyen, and S. Blachfellner, editors. *Systems Thinking: New Directions in Theory, Practice and Applications.* Inst. f. Telecooperation, Johannes Kepler University Linz, Austria, SEA-SR-41, March 2015	83
2016	M.C. Edson, G.S. Metcalf, P. Tuddenham, and G. Chroust, editors. *Systems Literacy - Proceedings of the Eighteenth IFSR Conversation 2016,* SEA-SR 47. Books on Demand, Norderstedt, Germany, Feb. 2017	106
2018	G.S. Gary S. Metcalf, M.C. Edson, and G. Chroust, editors. S y s t e m s : f r o m s c i e n c e t o p r a c t i c e - *Proceedings of the 19th IFSR Conversation 2018.* BoD - Books on Demand, Norderstedt, Germany, 2019. (to be published April 2019)	Ca 130

What is the IFSR ?

THE INTERNATIONAL FEDERATION FOR SYSTEMS RESEARCH (IFSR), founded 1981, is a non-profit, scientific and educational organization comprising 47 member organizations (status December 2018) from all continents, see http://www.ifsr.org/index.php/member-societies/. The IFSR has shown a healthy growth with respect to the number of members and activities.

The overall purpose of the Federation is to advance cybernetic and systems research and systems applications in order to serve the international systems community, as also spelled out in the constitution.

The Federation is guided by a Board of Directors, composed of one or two individuals from each member organization. The Board elects biennial a President, one to three Vice Presidents, and the Secretary General. These officers form the Executive Committee (EC). The EC acts for the Board pursuant to the authorization of the Board. The Board meets bi-annually in even years, the EC annually.

The IFSR utilizes the following major means of publication:

The Journal of Systems Research and Behavioral Science

The IFSR Book Series on Systems Science and Engineering

The IFSR Newsletter

Proceedings of Fuschl Conversations

The IFSR maintains a Web-site and informs subscribers by short pieces of information, the 'IFSR News Flash '.

Officers of the IFSR   (1980 - 2019)

Year	President	Vice-President(s)	Secretary/Treasurer
1980	George J. Klir	Robert Trappl	Gerard de Zeeuw
1984	Robert Trappl	Bela H. Banathy	Gerard de Zeeuw
1988	Gerrit Broekstra	Franz Pichler	Bela Banathy
1992	Gerard de Zeeuw	J.D.R. De Raadt	Gerhard Chroust
1994	Bela Banathy	Michael C. Jackson	Gerhard Chroust
1998	Michael C. Jackson	Yong Pil Rhee	Gerhard Chroust
2000	Yong Pil Rhee	Michael C. Jackson	Gerhard Chroust
2002	Jifa Gu	Matjaz Mulej, Gary S. Metcalf	Gerhard Chroust
2006	Matjaz Mulej	Jifa Gu, Gary S. Metcalf	Gerhard Chroust
2008	Matjaz Mulej	Yoshiteru Nakamori, Gary S. Metcalf	Gerhard Chroust
2010	Gary S. Metcalf	Kyoichi Jim Kijima, Amanda Gregory, Leonie Solomons	Gerhard Chroust
2012	Gary S. Metcalf	Yoshihide Horiuchi, Stefan Blachfellner	Gerhard Chroust
2014	Gary S. Metcalf	Stefan Blachfellner, Mary C. Edson, Nam Nguyen	Gerhard Chroust
2016	Mary C. Edson	Gary S. Metcalf, Jennifer Wilby, Ray Ison	Gerhard Chroust
2018	Ray Ison	Nam Nguyen, Louis Klein	Stefan Blachfellner

History of Conversations :
A picture Gallery

1982: Fuschl , Pension Seewinkel

Pension Seewinkel, detail

THE FUSCHL SYMPOSIUM '82

The first proceedings

1994

Gerhard Chroust, Bela H. Banathy

David Tamas
Bela H. Banathy
(courtesy G. Dyer)

2000

Gordon Dyer (courtesy G. Dyer)

Gordon Rowland
(courtesy G. Dyer)

Gordon Dyer,
Mrs. Ferstl

Advertising ing Hotel
Seewinkel

2000

Charles Francois, Arne
Collen, Gerhard Chroust

2002

Fritz Stallinger, Gordon Dyer

2002: Fuschl, Hotel Schlick

Yoshi Horiuchi, Ockie Bosch

Lake Fuschl

2006

Mieczyslaw Bazewicz, Allan Combs, Magdalena Kalaidjieva

2008

The Dining Room

Gerhard Chroust, Hertha Idinger

Hertha Idinger, Janie Chroust

?, Alexander Laszlo, Wolfgang Hofkirchner, ?, Allenna Leonard

2010: Schloss Pernegg

Ernesto Grun, Magnus Ramage

Katie Laszlo, Kahlia Laszlo

Günther Ossimitz, Gary Metcalf, Gordon Dyer, Magnus Ramage

Yoshi Horiuchi, Gordon Dyer, Gerhard Chroust, Sadaharu Ishida,, Leonie Solomons

2012 : St Magdalena, Linz

Group Music: Hilary Sillitto, Kahlia Lazslo, Alexander Laszlo, James Martin, Debora Hammond

Alexander Laszlo, Violeta Bulc, Ockie Bosch, Nam Nguyen

James Martin: ‚work done'

2014

Linz from St. Magdalena

Rick Adcopck, Janet Singer, Mike Yearworth, Michael Singer

Jed Jones, Yoshi Horiuchi, Gordon Rowland, Gordon Dyer, Silvia Zweifel

2016

Mary Edson, Gerhard Chroust, Vice Rector Alexander Egyed, Gary Metcalf

Florian Daniel, Gerhard Chroust, Gary Smith, Maria Castro de Lobo, Brigitte Allegro, Xijin Tang, Gordon Dyer

Gary Metcalf, Gerhard Chroust, Nam Nguyen, Mary Edson, Stefan Blachfellner, Tay Ison

Brigitte Allegro, Xijin Tang, Peter Tuddenham

2018

Shankar Sankaran, Allenna Leonard, Jennifer Wilby, Pamela Buckle

Gary Smith

Nam Ngyuen, Gary Smith

Andreas Hieronymi, von Mitschke-Collande Josephine , Mark Pierson, Thanh Van Nguyen, Olaf Brugman

Gary Smith, Swami Natarajan, Hillary Sillitto, Gary Metcalf, George Mobus, Jenni9fer Makar

Part II : IFSR Conversation 2018
Proceedings of the 2018 IFSR Conversation

Team 1: Systems Practice

Brugman, Olaf (ND)

Hieronymi, Andreas (CH)

Malik, Constantin (CH) [co-team coordinator]

Von Mitschke-Collande Josephine (CH)

Nguyen, Nam (AU/VN) [team coordinator]

Pierson, Marc (US)

Thanh Van Nguyen (VN)

Executive Summary

This report summarises the activities and outcomes of the Systems Practice Team (SPT) at the 2018 International Federation for Systems Research (IFSR) Conversation in Linz, Austria. The 2018 SPT consists of mainly systems practitioners: Dr Nam Nguyen (team coordinator), Dr Constantin Malik (co-team coordinator), Dr Olaf Brugman, Mr Andreas Hieronymi, Ms Joséphine von Mitschke-Collande, Asso. Prof. Dr Thanh Van Nguyen (Dr. Thanh) and Dr Marc Pierson.

The discussed topic (Systems Practice) is relevant to a new type of membership in the IFSR constitution. It is also 'close to hearts' of many systems scientists, whom would really like to take systems sciences more into practice.

This topic is also closely related and complementary to several recent IFSR Conversation topics, e.g. "Systems Research", "Systems Literacy" (an effort to educate/inform a broader audience about systemic approaches to research and practice).

The mSPT shared their experience of applying systems approaches in practice. The team also discussed how to make systems approaches, systems tools more applicable to their respective fields and practice, with specific cases such as public security, smart city and leadership development in Vietnam, community healthcare in the US, cyber-security in Europe, etc.

A systems model, capturing the key variables of Systems Practice, was developed. Systemic roles and interconnections of the variables were diagnosed, leading to the identification of several important 'leverage points' that could help enhancing the system.

The following sections describe the SPT's Conversation in more details.

Expectations for the week

These were shared among the SPT members and submitted in advance to the IFSR Conversation organisers:

- Sharing the various applications of systems approaches in practice
- Exploring the 'untouched' potentials of systems approaches in practice
- Discussing ways to make systems approaches become more applicable to practice
- Discussing the most effective ways of communicating the results of this conversation to different end-user audiences (e.g. other systems scientists, systems practitioners, decision makers in government and funders of projects)
- Forming an action plan of the team
- Finding synergies among practitioners to foster joint applications
- Identifying ways to make systems approaches the preferred solution for decision-makers

Brainstorming the Systems Practice 'landscape'

The SPT commenced with a brainstorming session of the Systems Practice 'landscape'.

To get familiar with the main topic of our team and also to explore the team members' thoughts and associations with the topic, an exploratory brainstorm was conducted with regard to the main topic: "Systems Practice". Ideas were individually generated and written on coloured sticky notes paper. Next, the group identified similarities and synonyms in the ideas laid out. Through a group conversation, the thoughts and associations were clustered around common topics, such as "learning", "practice", "leadership", "tools" etcetera (Figure 1). Also, the relationships between the ideas were explored and assessed. This procedure proved to be an inspiring pre-exercise to get to more formalised and structured modelling of our main topic and problem area, and also made the members familiar with the richness of each other's thinking. It paved the way for a faster and structure model building using the Sensimod tool, since all Team Members were already more familiar with each other's thinking.

Figure 1a: Systems Practice 'Brainstorming' (Photo Olaf Brugmann, 2018)

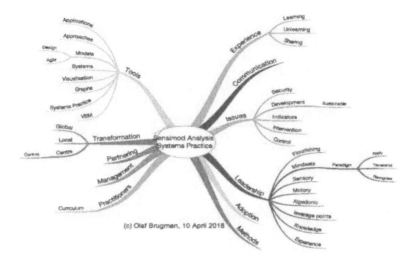

Figure 1b: Systems Practice 'Brainstorming'

Sharing Experiences and Applications

SPT members then shared their experiences and practical applications of systems approaches in various contexts and places, which included:

- Application of systems science in leadership and management on non-traditional security threats in Vietnam
- Application of systems science in building up smart cities meeting indicators of security–welfare–safety in the context of the 4th industrial revolution
- Malik SuperSyntegration for Smart Cities (Brainport Smart District, the Netherlands)
- Technical infrastructure for self-organizing in US counties
- Application of systems science for large scale societal transformation toward sustainability in Europe
- Experiences of applying systems thinking and gamification in educational setting
- Application of systems science at the national level for a community bank in Brazil
- The Art of Interconnected Thinking – Starting with the young (Malik simulation Ecopolicy program), in Germany, Australia and Vietnam
- Application of systems thinking for everyone

Key questions from the team

After the 'sharing' session, the SPT discussed further and posed some key questions on the ways moving forward:

- How can systems thinking and systems approaches help to address and prevent the emerging and non-traditional security issues and threats?
- How can systems thinking and systems approaches help to improve the indicators to manage smart cities for the need of safety, welfare and security?
- How can systems thinking and systems tools help to enhance effective leadership and management?
- How can we interconnect the key factors of 'Systems Practice' and identify the 'leverage points' for intervention and improvement?
- What are our next steps and actions?

Systems Practice: 14 key variables

Various elements were discussed and thought of as relevant factors to Systems Practice, which were then categorized into 14 key variables, namely:

1 Global transformation
2 Effectiveness of leadership and management
3 Sharing experience (inside)
4 Local transformation
5 Co-operation (inside)
6 Problems
7 Effective communication
8 Effective systems practice
9 Effectiveness of tools and methods
10 Effectiveness of indicators
11 Transformation control centre (TCC)
12 Flourishing (inside)
13 Ability to transcend paradigm
14 Systems training

Systems Model «Systems Practice» and the interconnection

The _Malik Sensitivity Model_ (SensiMod) was used to develop a causal loop diagram (systems model) of the key variables of Systems Practice (Figure 2). SensiMod is a very effective tool to find and visualize the inter-connectedness and dependencies of complex systems. With the computer based SystemTool it is easy to integrate insights about complex environments, markets, innovations, organizational culture and more. It is a powerful thinking-tool which enables the Systems Practice Team to grasp the complex system of "Systems Practice" holistically, to visualize its inter-connectedness and to get to know the dynamics and behaviour of this complex system. Consequently, it discloses the most powerful levers for controlling and steering the system into the desired direction, with lowest possible resource efforts.

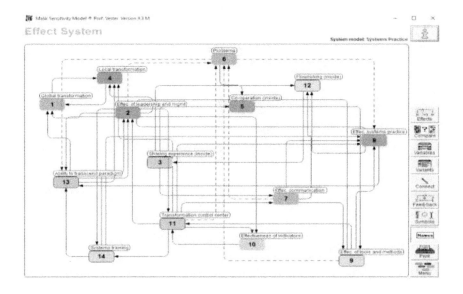

Figure 2: causal loop diagram (systems model) of the key variables of Systems Practice

⟶ : Confirming effect between two variables: The more/less, the more/less

: Opposing effect between two variables: The more/less, less/more

The diagram provides far more value than just the aforementioned 'list', Figure 2 illustrates the key topics of the systems practice discussion. The colors of the variables show their systemic roles (as discussed further in the following sections).

The systems model consists of 14 variables and 42 interrelations. There are 157 feedback loops with 125 reinforcing feedback loops and 32 stabilizing/balancing feedback loops. This system is strongly interconnected (degree of networking 3.00 = 20% more than average). Strong interconnection and the dominance of reinforcing feedback loops show that the *system can be activated*. However, for gaining active control of such a strongly interconnected system, single measures will not be sufficient. *Concerted and simultaneous intervention* at different parts of the system is needed.

Assessing strength of interconnection – Impact Matrix

The Impact Matrix (Figure 3) is used to assess the interaction between the relevant variables in the system context. This is essential because the role of a variable is never recognizable on its own, what important are the interactions between the variables.

An overview and common understanding of the strengths of the interactions are obtained by asking the question "If variable A changes, how does this change the direct effect on variable B?", rated with the values 0,1,2 or 3 (none, slight, proportional, or disproportionate relationship).

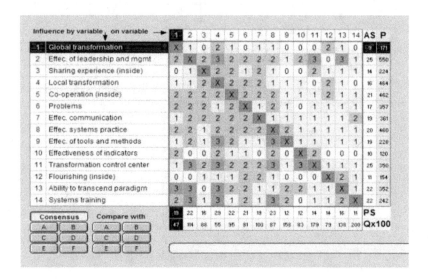

Figure 3: Impact Matrix of the key variables of Systems Practice
0: Strong change in variable A causes little or no change in variable B (A and B range from 1 to 14)
1: Strong change in A causes only a slight change in B
2: Change in A causes an equally strong change in B
3: Weak change in A causes a very strong change in B

'Rainbow' Effect Levers

Based on the impact matrix, the distribution of roles are created, effect on the variables is hereby clarified.

Due to the distribution of roles, the capabilities of the system and the cybernetic role of the variables are visible (Figure 4). This allows the assessment of the behaviors and influence of the overall system and of each variable. Various recommendations and findings can be obtained, such as:

- Where we can find possible control levers
- What are the components that can jeopardize the system
- What are the indicators that make good improvements to the system
- The nature of the system, respectively showing the behavior of the system (rigid, inert, stable, critical, volatile, ...)
- Identification of possible levers, indicators (measuring sensor) and critical points

We distinguish different variables:

Active variables: Variables in this area are the strongest drivers which significantly affect the system performance. They are therefore suitable - if directly influenced - as a shift lever. When you find the right approach, these variables can stabilize the system after a change.

Buffering variables: Area where interventions and controls serve no purpose. Unless its change affects very specifically an active component.

Critical variables: Variables in this area have a critical effect; they can lead to large positive or negative effects. They are suitable for "initial sparks", but have to be used carefully.

Neutral variables: These are highly interconnected variables (in relation to other variables). They are important for the self-regulation of the system.

Reactive variables: Variables in this field are system indicators which reflect the changes of the system. These variables are strongly dependent on other variables, but have a weak effect themselves.

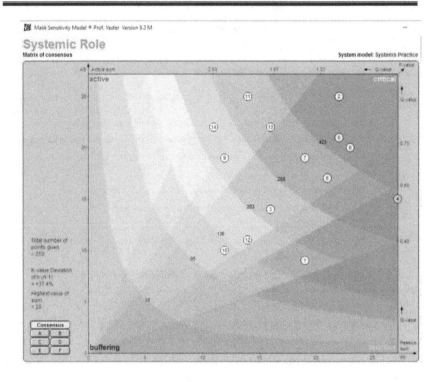

Figure 4: Systemic Role of the key variables of Systems Practice
(the numbers correspond to the tasks in Fig. 3)

"Effectiveness of leadership and management" is the most essential variable for moving the system «Systems Practice»

Results of models always depend on the quality of initial inputs. Based on the limited time available for building our model, we derived the following provisional insights. System diagnosis (Figure 5): "Effectiveness of leadership and management" is the variable that is part of the highest number of reinforcing feedback loops (105 of 125 = 80%). If it is deactivated, the number of reinforcing feedback loops is reduced to 16% (20 instead of 125). The system can only be activated if "Effectiveness of leadership and management" is achieved.

Critically important: "Effectiveness of leadership and management" will directly improve the status of nine variables in all parts of the system.

This essential variable is itself directly influenced by four other variables ('leverage points'), most importantly: "Systems training", "Transformation control center", "Ability to transcend paradigm" and "Effectiveness of tools and methods".

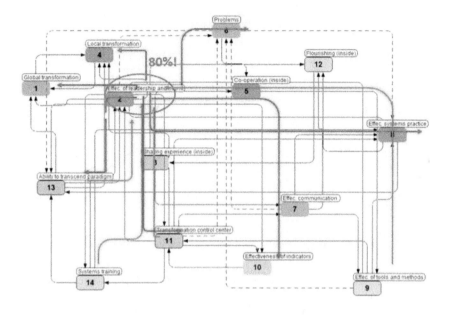

Figure 5: The most important variable of Systems Practice

Partial Scenario: Simulation

Given the time constraint, the SPT only undertook a partial scenario to see the possible impact of changing the 'leverage points' in the system on the most important variable (Figures 6 & 7).

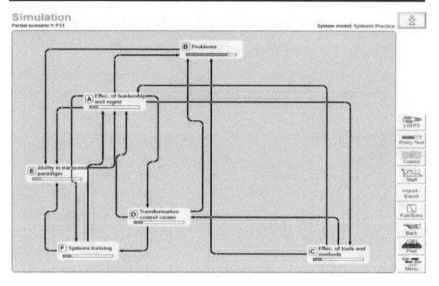

Figure 6: Partial scenario of Systems Practice ('current situation')
Colour of variable's status in status bar – red: not good; yellow: alarming; green: good

Small changes have big effects on the system: making small changes in the three leverage points (D, C, F), for only three rounds already enhances significantly the effectiveness of leadership and management (see Figures 6 & 7).

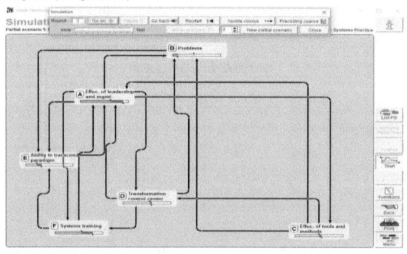

Figure 7: Partial scenario of Systems Practice (simulation after three rounds)
Colour of variable's status in status bar – red: not good; yellow: alarming; green: good

Key suggestions and actions

Below are some key recommendations of the Systems Practice Team:

1. Building a framework to steer, regulate and control the various issues that Dr. Thanh presented and the Ministry of Public Security (MPS) has to deal with;
2. The above framework could be used as a basis to further develop a Transformation Control Centre (TCC) – both for managing the non-traditional security issues and enhancing the smart cities indicators;
3. The TCC would have tools and systems that enable the leaders and managers to visualize the actions as they are happening, with real-time checking and controlling;
4. The Malik SuperSyntegration (MSS) methodology would also be useful to deal with the issues that Dr. Thanh presented (e.g. examples of MSS applications for Brainport Smart City in the Netherlands, Cybersecurity for one of the biggest finance and insurance companies in the world, etc);
5. It is also important to design the right customized training courses in systems thinking, systems tools, effective management, etc. in order to enhance the effectiveness of leadership and management.

Figure 8: Dr. Thanh – presenting and 'having fun' with the SP team members:
Andreas Hieronymi, Josephine von Mitschke-Collande Josephine , Constantin Malik, Thanh Van Nguyen, Marc Pierson, Olaf Brugman

All of the above will help to increase the impact that the leadership of MPS has on the Ministry. It will also have a self-re-enforcing positive effect among the people in MPS. Furthermore, the aforementioned actions would contribute to the global effort[*] of making systems thinking and

---

[*] *In 2017, the United Nations (UN), the World Health Organization (WHO) and the Organization for Economic Co-operation and Development (OECD) all publically declared systems thinking to be a key leadership skill that is necessary to deal with the fundamental interconnectedness of complex, local-to-global economic, social and environmental issues.*

systems approaches become more applicable to practice and the preferred solutions for decision-makers, managers and leaders.

Figure 8: Systems Practice Team ….

Figure 10: Systems Practice Team – social activity (on the top of Linz)

Systems Practice - the Art of Connected Thinking
Olaf Brugman
(individually contributed paper)

(reprinted from IFSR Newsletter vol. 35, no. 1, p. 18 – 15)

The IFSR Conversation 2018 on Systems Science was the first I participated in. It had proven to be an almost priceless opportunity to converse and work for a week with fellow-systems practitioners and to discuss, define and elaborate solutions for challenges in our societies. We worked on Systems Practice: how can we equip system practitioners with the collective system science skills to observe, understand and steer complex systems. We focused on social systems: organizations and networks of institutions, organizations and people: how do we define the purposes of such systems, how do we model them, how do we understand them and develop solutions? And more importantly even: how do we promote that we, systems practitioners, learn to further apply our skills, and how do we promote that complex systems have those skills available to their better functioning? In other words, we worked on both the professional and the systems level.

We were object and subject at the same time. We were observers and the observed. We were a dynamic, forming, learning, and intervening system at the same time. We derived our learning from public health, security, problem solving methods, deep reflection, and also from over 160 years of combined professional experience. And we applied our knowledge back to it.

Of the group of seven fellow-system practitioners in our working group, I already knew three of them and have had the pleasure to work with them before. This helped us as a group to get a head start in our proceedings. However, getting in touch with three new colleagues added new perspectives and options to the group, which I felt was very beneficial to all of us. It was striking how entering in conversations with well-intended colleagues whom I had not had the pleasure to work with before always leads to different understanding of systems, and new views on making them function better. Even more than expected.

The methods at least of the group members were familiar with were management cybernetics in the tradition of Stafford Beer, Fredmund Malik and others. And also with management cybernetics learning and problem solving methods based on Systems Practice for Everyone (Ockie Bosch, Nam Nguyen, Nguyen Van Thanh). We used these methods to formulate our leading questions, to model the complex systems dynamics and find solutions. What struck me exceptionally was the insight, from five days of conversations, that systems function is an outcome of a whole set of different factors: training and educating professionals, leadership, technology, health etc. And also how connected several aspects of our societies are - economy, environment, social relationships, climate, health, innovation, well-being, public security.

The conversations and group work led to some new and surprising insights. We were able to go beyond the usual training and educational approach visualizing how to enable professionals to develop their skills. Our methods led us to see that we can also look at how certain skills and qualities are available in the system, even if they are not present in each and every individual, such as monitoring, capacity increasing systems' responsiveness, and the interconnecting between economic, environmental and social factors all influence each other, representing both challenges and leverage points for solutions. Also, it became clear how difficult it is to arrive at new knowledge: complex social systems tend to reinforce around their current homeostats: governance structures, power structures, personal roles and individuals all work to maintain the status quo. Leaders and those in power who 'see' are not always able to 'speak' since the system may relentlessly fall unto them in an attempt to preserve the system.

Interactions with other groups or others we had relatively few, mainly because we as a group had several activities in the evening, and also since I had to take care of ongoing business concerns outside the Conversation hours. Therefore the opportunities for interaction were rather limited, or at least more than I had wanted. That was a missed opportunity, but it also enabled more in-depth learning on our working group's main theme.

All in all, the systems practice week in Linz, organized by the International Federation for the Systems Sciences (IFSR) was extremely rich and insightful, inspiring, and it deepened experiences that enhanced my skills as a systems practitioner. I am grateful to the event organizers and hosts, my working group's members and coordinators, the IFSR and also the wider group of the IFSR Conversations in Linz

====== **Report on the IFSR Conversation 2000 (excerpt)** ==========

Newsletter

The Official Newsletter of
THE INTERNATIONAL FEDERATION
FOR SYSTEMS RESEARCH

G. Chroust: Editor-in-Chief

VOLUME 20, No. 1 (SEPT 2001)

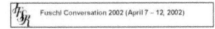

Fuschl Conversation 2002 (April 7 – 12, 2002)

Fuschl –20 Years history

Why conversation and what form do they take?

TEAM 2: "What is System Science"

Jennifer Makar (CA)
Gary Metcalf (US)
George Mobus (US)
Swami Natarajan (UK / IN)
Hillary Sillitto (UK)
Gary R Smith (UK)

Why the question of "What is Systems Science"?

- The purpose of the conversation
- Patterns of thought
- Ambitions for integration

The purpose of this conversation was to explore if we could make progress towards the unification of systems science as a coherent system. We felt that the time was right, since multiple perspectives, patterns in works of thought and practice from diverse sources and backgrounds indicated the potential of an emerging coherence. The motivation for the conversation was to determine if these various threads could somehow be woven together into a more integrated understanding, and to make progress towards the unification of systems science as a coherent systematic enterprise. We believe that systems science is analogous to where chemistry was before the Periodic Table of the elements: many phenomena have been described, many of them understood as individual concepts and theories, but this knowledge is not yet integrated around a single foundational structure. The systems community have developed and applied some very effective systemic methodologies (e.g. Soft Systems Methodology, System Dynamics, Viable System Model, Architectural Frameworks and others) in several fields like systems engineering (INCOSE), Operational Research, Organisational Design and research. But without a unifying framework that everyone can refer to for understanding and communication, our ability to teach, develop coherently and practice system science has been limited. With a more unified system science, we may create sufficient coherence to address the global systemic issues confronting humankind and our future on this planet.

We proposed therefore a conversation to progress towards the unification of systems science as a coherent system.

Our team: Gary Metcalf, George Mobus, Swami Natarajan, Jennifer Makar, Hillary Sillitto and Gary Smith.

If you ask people what "systems science" is, even as an abstraction, you will hear many different interpretations. In order to develop a shared understanding and consensus, our conversation team endeavored to take into account diverse stakeholder perspectives, needs and experience. It was important that what was created or arose from this conversation was presented as a proposal. We aimed to initially create a working consensus as to what systems science is, so we can then apply systems approaches to identify and arrange the required concepts into an **architecture** that will provide the necessary structure for our collective knowledge and practice of the science. Within this framework the methods of systems science and systems practices might then be integrated as a more complete system. Methods from systems science and approaches were applied as an aid to the conversation and drew on the experience of the team.

One particular pattern in which we had found inspiration prior to the conversation was across diverse perspectives, practices and theories about systemic transformations. In the diagram below, concepts within perspectives and frameworks such as Cynefin (Snowden 2000) and DRSP (Cabrera and Colosi 2008) are laid out across the rows and organised within columns that are arranged from what might be considered 'blue sky thinking' to ' real world thinking'. Within this framework if you look up and down the columns, it is possible to see interesting and possibly useful relationships across these different perspectives..

Abstract / Intangible	Abstract / Organised	Tangible / Organised	Tangible / Controlled
Visualise Systems	Appreciate Systems	Plan Systems	Operate Systems
Distinctions	Structure	Relationships	Perspectives
Information	Knowledge	Force/Interactions	Mass/Energy
Conceptualisation	Architecture	Design	Implementation
Philosophy	Science	Engineering	Realisation
Perceived Chaos	Perceived Complexity	Perceived Complicated	Perceived Obvious
Observe Why	Orient / Appreciate What	Decide How	Act / Utilise
Hypothesis	Theory	Principle	Law

For instance, imagine a situation of great surprise, someone been blindfolded unexpectedly, they have been spun around, moved from place to place, they are dazed and confused and suddenly the blindfold has been removed. They receive information from their senses, at that instant of their eyes seeing, without a clear framework, everything seems confused, everything initially appears as chaos, distinctions of things are made, systems are visualised within this context but nothing makes sense yet within the whole. In starting to make sense of what it observed, hypothesis are drawn, compared to thoughts about why, and suddenly there is then the eureka moment, it makes sense, 'its a birthday party'. 'Now I can appreciate it....'

The table is far from complete but we have looked at many other philosophies and found that an integration of concepts can be achieved and is often revealing. In the conceptualisation of this conversation we knew that critical to making progress was an appreciation and integration of diverse philosophies and that being able to make connections and see patterns gave us hope for an integrative framework.

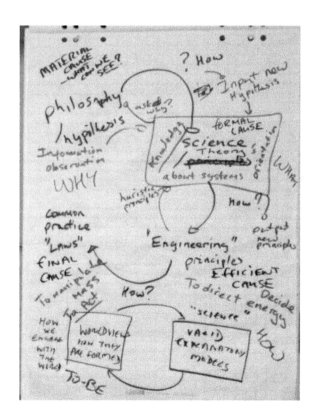

To date, the systems engineering community has established a practice that supports the **realisation** of systems. The transformation of systems through perceived chaos, perceived complexity, perceived complicatedness and perceived obvious, reflects a real world experience but lacks the connection to system science foundations. In this conversation we envisioned systems practitioners and systems scientists to begin to identify and collate the methods to analyse and trace the systemic concepts (or elements) utilised such as hierarchy, structure, components, values etc.

Through a shared **conceptualisation** and **architecture** for a system of system science we hope to integrate our concepts and methods into an overall system **design** that will greatly increase our ability to more successfully interact with systems and their environments. In doing so, systems science can be more effectively **realised**, applied and advanced.

A diversity of world views on systems
(Hillary Sillitto)

- (Why do we see systems and live in systems.)
- Why do people have different viewpoints of what systems are and what are the advantages of these?
- Bridging the schism

In recently published research, (Sillitto, Griego et al. 2018) established that there are at least seven distinct, and to a considerable extent mutually incompatible, worldviews on systems within a relatively small population of systems engineering experts in the INCOSE Fellows' and System Science Working Group (SSWG) communities.

The worldviews identified ranged from constructivist ("systems are purely a mental construct") to "extreme realist" ("systems only exist in the real world"). Some considered the threshold of "systemicity" to be as simple as "two or more inter-related elements"; while others demanded a wide range of attributes, including those of living systems, before considering something to be a system.

That such a wide range of worldviews was discovered within the Systems Engineering community was a surprising result. We might expect to find an even wider range of worldviews across a more diverse community; but a non-rigorous examination of the results of the survey and of the wider literature suggests that the range of "system" worldviews held by the surveyed group of Systems Engineers is broadly representative of the systems field as a whole – and much wider than would probably have been expected from that group, given the relatively narrow perceived focus of Systems Engineering within the overall scope of systemology.

Comparing the scope of the survey reported by (Sillitto, Griego et al. 2018) to (Rousseau and Billingham 2018) "Systematic Framework for Exploring Worldviews", the survey focused on the ontology, metaphysics and axiology aspects of respondents' belief systems, and did not explore the cosmology, praxeology or (to any significant extent) the epistemology perspectives.

The INCOSE Fellows have all been recognised by their peers as eminent and successful people in their field; so it did not seem possible to discount any of the worldviews held by these individuals as "wrong". (Extending the survey to the Systems Science Working group did not increase the number of worldviews identified.) It was necessary therefore to adopt the position that all worldviews discovered are valid perspectives on systems, and are useful within particular domains of practice. Having observed this community at work, Sillitto (2016) observes that worldview differences do not prevent effective collaboration on practical tasks.

So, according to this evidence, and contrary to prior expectation, **a group of people working together on the same systemic topic will not necessarily share a common worldview on systems**. It is often sufficient for members of the group to act "as if" a certain worldview is valid regarding a specific situation and the use of a specific practice. However, if we seek a deeper understanding of the nature of systems, and the way they are perceived by humans - for example to clarify, improve and make use of systems science – we need to understand

a) that divergent worldviews are likely to inhibit agreement on what can be considered to be "true", "relevant", and "universal" about the field;

b) and conversely, if multiple worldviews are not represented when a consensus is being built, that consensus will not survive contact with the worldviews not represented when it was established.

Sillitto et al (2018) go on to discuss the applicability of the different worldviews they identified to different aspects of Systems Engineering. Their work has led to a revised set of definitions being proposed to INCOSE for various types of "system" of interest to systems engineers, with a strong focus on ensuring the definitions themselves would be at least approximately acceptable to a wider community. The IFSR 2018 conversation was itself an opportunity to test this acceptability; though the proposed definitions were not explicitly presented and discussed, the conversation influenced the thought process.

The work on identifying and characterising different worldviews focused our team on:

a) the need for a wide consideration of system types, including simple and complex, physical and conceptual;

b) the need to "bridge the schism" between the constructivist and the realist worldviews.

Most systems engineers would probably place themselves in the "moderate realist" camp, if only because systems engineers have to be fluent at moving between the conceptual space, when they are doing exploration and design, and the physical space when they are doing real-world implementation. However many eminent and thoughtful systems engineers are constructivists; while other systems engineers are extreme realists, and consider that Systems Engineering must move towards the biological metaphor for engineered systems. Systems Engineering needs both perspectives, and if it is to integrate them successfully, needs input from systems science on both perspectives.

A position where different worldviews represent competing belief systems, of which only one can be "right", will not bridge the schism. We seek a synthesis, in which different worldviews represent different valid perspectives on a single more complex universe of systems. This would allow us to choose appropriate tools, techniques and mind-sets from different worldviews, as required to address a specific problem.

The key issue, and an important learning from the Conversation, is that when systems people come together to work together on fundamental topics:

a) we are all trapped, to a greater or lesser extent, within our own worldviews, and the largely unspoken and often unrecognised assumptions that underpin them;

b) the differences between our and others' worldviews may by much more profound that any of us realise;

c) unless we explicitly explore them, we will be largely unaware of others' worldviews, and how we may be using the same words for subtly or very different concepts.

Perhaps most important, we can't expand one worldview to properly address key concepts that are foundational to other worldviews. We need to bridge across worldviews at a "meta-level", rather than try to generalise from one world view in the hope that it can "sort of" accommodate others. We need a "meta-framework" that preserves the coherence of each separate worldview, while showing us how to integrate across the different worldviews to achieve a synthesis.

An excellent metaphor for this is wave-particle duality in Physics. Some experiments suggested that both electricity and light behaved as waves; while other experiments suggested that both electricity and light behaved like particles. Only after many decades of fruitless argument about "which was right" did physicists accept, early in the 20thCentury, that "both were right". Mathematical models were developed that, by varying the boundary conditions, correctly predicted the outcome of experiments involving both "wave" and "particle" behaviour; and physicists learned to understand when the wave approximation was more appropriate, and when the participle one was more useful. Acceptance of wave-particle duality paved the way for modern electronic and optical engineering. Without it, now-pervasive technologies including digital cameras, electronic displays, and solar panels would not exist.

We conclude that Systems Science would benefit greatly if it can consider and achieve a synthesis across the apparently conflicting worldviews of constructivism and realism, expressed in terms of these two key aspects:

a) the nature of systems in the physical universe; and

b) the way humans perceive and interact with systems.

A diversity of knowledge about systems
(Gary Metcalf)

- Utility of General Systems Theory
- Isomorphism across knowledge bases
- Appreciating the value of diverse philosophies

(Von Bertalanffy 1968) defined three "aspects" of systems theory. Systems **science** is the "scientific exploration and theory of 'systems' in the various sciences (e.g. physics, biology, psychology, social sciences), and general system theory as doctrine of principles applying to all (or defined subclasses of) systems". Systems **technology** is the realm of "problems arising in modern technology and society, comprising both the 'hardware' of computers, automation, self-regulating machinery, etc. and the 'software' of new theoretical developments and disciplines". Finally, systems **philosophy** refers to the "reorientation of thought and world view ensuing from the introduction of 'system' as a new scientific paradigm (in contrast to the analytic, mechanistic, one-way causal paradigm of classical science)".

While this is not a universal set of distinctions with which all systems scientists or systems engineers would agree, it is a useful framework. At the least, the distinctions can help to explain some of the disagreements and misunderstandings that occur with respect to defining "systems."

What Bertalanffy defines as systems science is the most familiar realm to those involved in professional systems organizations, or in the development of systems theories. This situates systems concepts within or alongside disciplinary science. Applied to existing disciplines, it incorporates principles such as feedback and emergence. It emphasized understanding the properties of whole entities in the context of their environments, as opposed to entities only as composites of elements.

There is also a strong concern in systems about the "silos" which had developed between traditional disciplines, and the lack of abilities between scientists to collaborate, or often even to communicate with each other, due to different uses of terms and theories. At the highest level of organization, this led to the quest for a "general system theory" as the unification of science; one domain of science comprised of the most universal theories. At another level was the search for isomorphies which would cross many or most disciplines.

What (Von Bertalanffy 1968) called systems technology is most related to a "systems approach" (or indeed systems engineering) (p. 4), which implies an understanding and application of general principles, most like what is referred to as "systems thinking." It is actually the most familiar in terms of prevalence, but may not be associated with "systems" for everyone who uses it.

The three examples below illustrate increasing levels of complexity, and increasing interdependence with the environment of the system. Simple problems are often straightforward. They may require high levels of technical skill or expertise, but all of the relevant factors can be identified and assessed. More complex problems involve more complexity and ambiguity. The most complex problems cannot be solved with a final, optimal solution. They can be managed in relation to chosen goals, but will continue to evolve over time.

An engineer designing a new passenger jet might begin with many standard assumptions, for instance, that a jet airplane requires a fuselage, wings, tail section, engines, etc. A "new" jet might involve a new engine type, or possibly more automated navigation. Other assumptions might include that the jet will take off and land from airports having long runways and air traffic controllers.

Designing a new civil aviation vehicle (e.g. a "flying car") is a different kind of challenge. Many of the same principles of aeronautics still apply, and most of the needed information could ultimately come from user requirements. The users and the transportation systems involved, though, would multiply in complexity. There would be many "nested systems" to be considered. Deciding how to select the relevant systems and what the optimal view of relationships and hierarchies between them would be would involve both engineering expertise and human decision-making.

Creating a healthcare system is yet a greater order of complexity. There are many possible configurations, all of which offer different possibilities. Some might minimize costs; others might maximize individual longevity of life; still others might focus on quality of life, or on public health. The point is that the individuals involved understand something of the interconnected, and sometimes counter-intuitive, nature of the phenomena that they have to work with.

Systems philosophy is probably the least familiar, and the most challenging, to the majority of "Western thinkers." As discussed amongst the participants of this Conversation team, it is much less foreign to science as a whole than when Bertalanffy and other early systems scientists were writing. As noted, the only "unification" of science that was considered to be legitimate in the first half of the 20th century was the reduction of all science to the principles of physics. Despite the fact that quantum mechanics ultimately transformed physics in the first half of the 20th century, the expectations set by "physics-based" science in other realms were still largely those of a Newtonian, mechanical universe.

Brian Arthur, an economist and one of the early founders of the Santa Fe Institute, captured the spirit of the differences well in relation to complexity:

> You can look at the complexity revolution in almost theological terms, he says. "The Newtonian clockwork metaphor is akin to standard Protestantism. Basically there's order in the universe... If we act as individuals in our own right, if we pursue our own righteous self-interest and work hard, and don't bother other people, then the natural equilibrium of the world will assert itself. Then we get the best of all possible worlds—the one we deserve. That's probably not quite theological, but it's the impression I have of one brand of Christianity. The alternative—the complex approach—is total Taoist. In Taoism there is no inherent order. The world started with one, and the one became two, and the two became many, and the many led to myriad things.

The universe in Taoism is perceived as vast, amorphous, and ever-changing. You can never nail it down. The elements always stay the same, yet they're always rearranging themselves. So it's like a kaleidoscope: the world is a matter of patterns that change, that partly repeat, but never quite repeat, that are always new and different (Waldrop 2008)

Bertalanffy referenced the process philosophy of Whitehead, along with Gestalt theory, and the role of the "observer" in human perception and understanding. The concepts that he presented align most naturally with what have been described as "Eastern views," in which reality is not a fixed representation that deteriorates over time, but an ever-flowing process containing more or less stable patterns, making up the entities that we experience each day in the world.

What is useful from "Science" and what would System Science be useful for

(George Mobus)

- Key questions for system science
- Complications and Patterns
- Bringing things together

There are currently a number of efforts underway to define systems science. There have been ongoing conversations within IFSR Conversation teams addressing various aspects of systems science-quo-science. INCOSE has a working group doing essentially the same thing with an effort to describe an 'ontology' of systems as a basis for a language for describing systems in various forms (but especially for designed systems). Rousseau, et. al. is working on finding scientific principles (as opposed to heuristic principles) through a rigorous process.

Our 2018 Conversation team addressed two tightly related questions in this respect. Our objective was to provide some more robust definition of what systems science is but this necessitated examining what was the subject matter of the science - what are the attributes, properties, principles, and theories that define something as being a system. Then, how are systems to be studied scientifically. So the two questions became: What is systemness? and What kind of science pertains to its study?

The question of what is systemness is particularly problematic. It is complicated by both philosophical and technical issues. According to the work done by Sillitto, et al, (2018) there are a number of worldviews on what constitutes the reality of systemness, from radical constructivists (who view systemness as a strictly human mental construct) to radical realists (who view systemness as a property of reality), and several milder forms in between. For much of the discussion our team tended toward a synthesis of these views, allowing that systemness is indeed constructed by human mental mechanisms during perception as a result of learning. Perception and reasoning to construct a view of something is subject to preconceptions, perspective, and lack of complete information. Different people can construct different mental models of a thing of observation and hence give rise to the suspicion that the systemness perceived is just a construction of the mind. However we allowed that another, and more reasonable position is that while this kind of mental construction goes on in the process of learning about a thing or phenomenon, for example, that there is a real basis in systemness in the observable universe. The ideal of systems perception would be that the mental model one holds converges in form on the real thing in the world. One possible way to reconcile this idea, allowing both constructivist and realist views to be consistent is to recognize that the human brain/mind is, itself a system that is preconditioned to perceive the properties of and patterns in systems (real things in the world) in order to make sense of the world. There is an evolutionary argument that having a brain that is predisposed to see systemness would enhance the fitness of the possessor so would be selected for in the course of brain evolution. One of us (Mobus) has hypothesized that the so-called language of thought (LoT) proposed by linguists and philosophers of mind (also referred to as mentalese) is actually a language based on systemness, that is, the brain constructs concepts and concept complexes (like spoken language sentences) using template patterns based on attributes of systemness. The conversation team found this useful and the discussion of what some of those attributes might be and how we might define systemness conditioned much of the discussion of what a systems science might be. We considered the traditional definition of what constitutes being a science, using, primarily, physical sciences such as physics, chemistry, and biology as providing the basic structure of a science. There is an old joke in these sciences that claims that if a subject domain needs to include the word 'science' in its name (social science, computer science, political science) then it is most likely not a science. We addressed some of the key capabilities necessary to consider system science as a science in the tradition of the physical sciences. For example, one of the key attributes of a science is that its theories should produce predictions about future behaviors of the things and phenomena it covers. Many of the explicitly labeled sciences (in parenthesis above) have demonstrated difficulty in this regard. Computer science, for example, should really be understood as applied mathematics.

Related to this is the question of how "scientific" systems science is at the moment, and how it might become "more scientific". (pp. 63-64 of: (Gauch Jr 2012)) summarises a debate about the rationality of science that appeared in in Physics Today in 1996-97 as follows.

"Seven lines of evidence were cited to show that science has a strong grip on the nature of reality:

1. steadily improving predictions, often unambiguous, precise, diverse, and even surprising;
2. increasingly accurate and extensive data;
3. increasingly specific and comprehensive theories;
4. interlocking evidence of diverse sorts;
5. progress over time in describing and explaining nature;
6. reproducible experiments; and
7. science-based technology (practice? architectures? techniques? "stuff"? Enablement? interventions?) that works.

Of those seven witnesses to science's success, the first, predictive power, was the strongest evidence that the natural sciences have an objective grip on reality." (With thanks to David Rousseau for identifying this source)

An additional complicating issue with talking about the study of systems as a science is that its subject matter is not any specific substance or class of phenomena, but general patterns of structures, functions, and behaviors that are found in the subject objects in the other sciences regardless of the specifics of their substrate substances. The other sciences have evolved rich sets of methodologies and techniques for exploring their subjects rigorously (e.g. precision measurements and mathematics) and empirically (propose falsifiable hypotheses regarding expectations, then confirm or disconfirm through some combination of experimentation, as in particle physics, and observation, as in astronomy). They assemble a body of established facts and synthesize them in the form of theories (The Standard Model, The Atomic Theory, and Evolution for physics, chemistry, and biology respectively). In this sense, systems science is dependent on the other sciences to do the actual discovery of relations and expose the patterns. But then, how should system science proceed to study such patterns and produce a set of principles and theories about systemness itself? One very useful move in this direction has been the categorization of patterns of processes, called "isomorphies" by Lenard Troncale and associates. These are patterns of behavior that can be found operating in a wide array of phenomenal processes. For example, the concept of a boundary (a concept the team spent no small amount of time tossing back and forth!) appears an identifiable phenomena in physics, chemistry, and biology, but also in sociology. We ask if boundaries are real things (or processes) or constructions of human choice? That question is probably still unresolved (or at least not completely bounded...) for the time being though there are strong opinions on both sides (as with constructivist vs. realist arguments). The point is, that the concept of a boundary or boundary conditions, appears applicable across all disciplinary domains when trying to isolate a system from its context/environment. In our discussions, we did agree on a partial reconciliation in terms of what might be called an "effective" boundary or the property of boundedness. Another attribute of a boundary, proposed, is a discontinuity in levels of entropy or organization wherein within a system effective boundary there is lower entropy as compared with the environment. This seems to have some definitional power but it remains unclear as to how the two entropies might be measured and just how much of a discontinuity (e.g. sharpness of a gradient identifiable, for instance in physically bounded systems) counts as determining that a boundary exists. It is possible that one fruitful track for systems science to take would be in exploring these kinds of questions. Are all systems bounded either by richer internal connections as compared with external ones, or some form of concrete boundary structure (e.g. a cell membrane), or some other kind of mechanism that allows the observer to distinguish between the system and its environment? This kind of research might be a legitimate thing for a true systems science to pursue.

The natural sciences seem to go through stages of development (we encourage the reader to reflect on the transformation table as you consider the following passage). The first stage is that of observation and description of interesting phenomena (dating back at least to ancient Mesopotamia and the agricultural revolution). At some point, natural philosophers note similarities and differences in phenomena and began to organize a classification scheme to categorize these aspects. The similarities and differences come increasingly to depend on measurements of attributes (size, position, speed, weight, etc.), which are themselves comparisons with some relevant standard for the measure. Eventually the science develops concepts, principles, and theories to explain the phenomena. And using the theories, they are able to predict what one should expect to observe under "interesting" conditions. This is the status of the domain of physical and chemical sciences today. Biology has entered this stage with the advent of genomic studies.

Systems science may be characterized as a discipline in transition from the descriptive stage to the categorization (organisation/architecture) stage. Even though people like von Bertalanffy posited a general systems theory - a mathematical structure not unlike the theory of gravity - the field has produced a number of descriptions, e.g. Viable Systems Theory, Living Systems Theory, that purport systemness, but actual mathematical theories that support prediction have yet to emerge. Specific subdisciplines of systems science, such as cybernetics and information theory, have produced theoretical bases that meet the test of scientific theory, but the fact that they are just pieces of the larger systems project does not translate into systems science having a comprehensive theoretical framework.

Without an integrative framework for organising our knowledge, it might be fair to say that systems science is to a degree stuck in the descriptive (naturalist) stage in the development of a science. In some ways akin to field biologists discovering new kinds of plants and animals prior to the development of a categorical science in which the characteristics of those various kinds could be compared and contrasted in various measurements, those biologists were caught in a process of describing similarities, yet over time seeing patterns that hinted at new possibilities of organisation.

The latter gave rise to the concept of relatedness and finally the Binomial Nomenclature system (now the cladistics system) and the ordering of groups of living things into kingdoms, phyla, classes, etc., the basis of our modern concepts of evolutionary descent. A major question we face is: Can system science get beyond this stage and is there a natural categorical structure (or structures) like the Periodic Table for chemistry that will help organize the body of knowledge about systemic patterns? Troncale's Systems Process Theory (Troncale 1978; Friendshuh and Troncale 2012) and collection of isomorphies provides a wealth of information but it has not yet been utilised within a knowledge structure with the explanatory power reminiscent of the Periodic Table or the Standard Model (Troncale 2013). The questions regarding what is systemness are addressed in the section below regarding system ontology, a subject we spent a fair amount of time discussing. As to the question of what constitutes systems science, we consider it still a very open one. Any review of the body of knowledge of systems science soon reveals a very disparate collection of ideas and observations but little in the way of trajectories toward definitive principles and theories developed in the traditional scientific way. We have a multitude of "systems-approaches" treaties such as Viable Systems Theory, Living Systems Theory, Soft Systems Theory, Cybernetics, and many more that describe phenomena that are discerned widely in physics, chemistry, biology, and sociology, but no overarching set of principles and theories that are specifically systems and derived from, for example, General Systems Theory . During the Conversation the team developed a preliminary framework that might serve as an organizing structure in the same way the Periodic Table has served chemistry. We applied some preliminary attempts at organizing various elements, initially borrowed from Troncale's isomorphies just to get a "feel" for how this framework (described elsewhere in this report) might come together. At the close of the Conversation we agreed that the basic start had been made but that much more discussion and working on the framework would be needed before we could say that we actually saw the "light at the end of the tunnel" with respect to what a systems science actually is.

Ontological Foundations for Systems
(George Mobus)

- Naming the things that exist
- How the universe organises itself

A key aspect of grappling with the concept of systemness is establishing what exists in our phenomenal universe – the substance(s) out of which systems are constructed. We need to identify the span of existing fundamental elements that comprise the construction. For example, we need to specify that something called a "component" exists and how a set of components relate to one another, the existence of relations to form a system. Additionally we need to consider what 'process' accomplishes that construction. In our Conversation we considered questions of ontological commitments (premises about what exists) and what the nature of ontogeny (the construction of new things) might entail. One of our conversants had recently finished writing a chapter for a new book and that chapter directly addressed some of these issues, so formed the basis for the discussion that ensued.

A system ontology needs to establish a set of terms naming those "things" that exist and a system ontogeny needs to describe a natural process whereby those things interact to form something that has the attributes of systemness. We started by considering the natural evolution of the Universe that has taken place from the Big Bang through the construction of nuclei, atoms, molecules, living cells, and up to, over the span of the 14+ billion year history of the Universe, human societies. These are the natural levels of organization and complexity. We noted, also, that the ontogenic process had to run counter to the general understanding of the 2nd law of thermodynamics.

The process of ontogenesis involves components at some level of organization having the capacity to form interactions, e.g. atoms can form molecules under the right conditions (context) and supply of free energy (in this case Gibbs free energy). Some such combinations may prove stable under the conditions, some may not. But of the ones that are stable they demonstrate emergent properties and interaction potentials due largely to new configuration geometries that permit new combinations. As the context evolves, e.g. the universe cooled and gravity accumulated galaxies, stars, and planets, some of these new possible combinations are realized and lead to a higher level of organization (e.g. nucleogenesis in stars gave rise to atoms and geochemistry gave rise to organic chemistry early primitive metabolism in planets and, at least on Earth, in the origin of life, (Smith and Morowitz 2016) Ontogenesis is described in (Mobus and Kalton 2015) (chapters 10 and 11). "Combogenesis" is a very similar process as described in (Volk 2017) who uses it to describe the "grand sequence" of increasing levels of organization/complexity. (Morowitz 2002) also describes this same universal evolution from simplicity to complexity. (Miller 1978) conveys the same basic message. Simple things can interact to form systems; those systems that are stable and successful in their environments go on to form new interactions; and the process repeats.

A full accounting for what systemness entails and how it can provide an explanatory model of what we observe in the universe today is needed to formulate a basis for a systems science. Some inroads have been made, but a fuller integration of many different threads of systems properties and functions has yet to be accomplished.

There have been several activities within INCOSE to try to define an ontology for systems. The Systems Science Working Group (SysSciWG) has been grappling with this through philosophical approaches while the OntoWG has been tackling it from the perspective of the approach taken in the WWW Consortium community wherein ontological definitions are focused on the needs of identifying objects in various subject domains (e.g. medicine) and coding how they are related. We might call this a "technological" approach to ontology as opposed to the more traditional "philosophical" approach.

The discussion in Linz centered on the idea that if systems are realities in the world, then the philosophical approach might be the more appropriate approach. However as one of us has pointed out (Sillitto) it is likely that any universal ontology should at least correspond with technological ontologies, for example with Basic Formal Ontology (BFO) formulations.

We began with a review of commitments about the most fundamental elements of the real world observed by quantum physics, categorized into "matter" (quarks and electrons) and "energy (photons). But we also discussed the ontological status of "knowledge" and "information" as ethereal but nevertheless causal substances [1]. There appears to be a symmetry in a cosmology based on a four quadrant model of substances, namely the well-known relation between matter and energy embodied in Einstein's famous equivalence equation, $E = mc^2$, is reflected in a similar equivalence relation between information and knowledge, e.g. knowledge, K is equal to the inverse of information, I ($K = 1/I$) wherein I is the amount of a priori uncertainty about the configuration (symbol) of a to-be received message[2]. The simple statement of this relation is that the more the receiver "knows" about the state of the sender the less information is provided by the receipt of the message. The receiver is less surprised as a result of a message and thus less informed.

Moreover, there is a relational symmetry between knowledge and matter, namely that the organization of some material object is its knowledge of the environment. And such a symmetry exists between energy and information. The latter is conveyed to the physical (material) object by the receipt of energy. In other words messages are conveyed by energetic flows (encoded as pulses, for example). The receipt of such flows by a receiving material object may then cause structural changes in it because the message states were not expected and, hence, informational. And the object's structure is physically changed as a result. Namely, the object becomes more dissipative of any such future message (this mechanism is presented in (Mobus and Kalton 2015) (Chapter 7).

The ontological commitments being proposed, then, are that there exists fundamental material substance, e.g. quarks and electrons, fundamental energy, e.g. bosons like photons, fundamental organizational structures in matter, e.g. knowledge, and fundamental causes of transformations, e.g. information. And there is an ontological process whereby at every level of organization these four substances interact in a dynamic universe to produce increasingly complex systems, first atoms, then molecules, etc. The epitome of emergent structures and functions is the societies of human beings (or any sentient beings anywhere in the Universe). Human brains are the epitome of complexity and organization emerged from biological evolution and the interactions between those brains as well as their autonomous agency (producing inventions of culture) produces the most complex systems in the Universe. Human society may be characterized as the (possibly transient) lowest entropy organization of which we know.

An ontological framework for developing a systems ontology was presented (Mobus, in preparation) and initial responses were favorable among the members of the team. The framework (not dissimilar to the BFO mentioned above) establishes a fundamental set of relations between concepts of systemness and provides a way to generate a language of systems. In this case we are talking about the possibility of a formal modeling language that might reflect the systemese discussed previously. Such a language would bridge the gap between the constructivists' conception of systems and the realists' views. The hypothesis is that the language of systems in the mind and a formal lexicon, semantics, and pragmatics can be brought together as a kind of Rosetta stone translation between our mental conceptualizations and realizations in models (specifically computerized dynamic models). A language of systems might serve as a means of translating concepts between disciplinary domains since a system property or attribute or "thing" would have a corresponding property, attribute, of object in the subject domain. A capacitor (and its charge) is not really different from a water reservoir (and its capacity). Flows of electrons are more than just analogous to flows of streams. A systems ontology and the subsequent description of a system language may provide for a means to achieve transdisciplinary communications after all.

Reflections on the nature of Systems

(Hillary Sillitto)

- Real world observables and model world abstractions
- Is "Systemness" a fundamental organising principle of nature?
- A grand sequence of systemicity and emerging periodicity

One aspect of systems science is understanding how to use "systems as models" to engage with complex "problem situations". The other, and perhaps more contentious, aspect, is understanding "systems in the physical universe", and the associated "scientific realist" worldview.

(Cabrera and Colosi 2008) distinguished between "real" and "conceptual" systems. The former exist in the physical universe, while the latter are mental constructs. (Rosen 2012) mirrors this with his Modelling Relation. Systems in the natural universe (which he called "natural systems") can be encoded as "formal systems" (i.e. models), while formal systems can be "decoded" into "natural" systems. As an aside, the label "natural systems" is problematic, because it is now widely used to refer to "naturally occurring systems", to distinguish them from human-made systems. A recent INCOSE (2018) study recommended using the term "physical system" for systems in the physical universe, including biological systems.

Thus, physical systems are composed of matter and energy. Their behaviour may manifest itself as flows of material, energy and information, and/or interaction through force fields. Information in physical systems is stored and transported in material/energy carriers (of which DNA is an example). The emergent property by which physical systems can be identified is that they transform matter, energy and information in ways that their individual parts cannot. Our knowledge of physical systems is ultimately limited by what can be observed, and is further limited by what observations we have chosen to make. Our understanding of physical systems is inevitably partial, and "is expressed as models and narratives" (Allen and Starr 2017).

[53]

IFSR Conversation 2018

Models are inherently incomplete, and are essentially "closed" systems. The physical systems they represent are invariably more or less open, and therefore subject to influences that may not be correctly represented in the model. Models, if they are to use useful in real world interventions, must always be validated, to understand whether, how well, and under what conditions, they characterise the physical systems they purport to represent.

Rosen emphasises the concept of "observables" as the linkage point between real systems and models. An observable is not the same as an observation. "Observability" of a real system does not mean it is being, or has been observed. It simply requires information about the system's state and effects to be accessible, in principle, to a notional sensor or "meter". What is observed depends a) on what an "observer" can, and chooses to, measure; and b) (as Allen and Starr emphasise) on the scale of the measurement.

This matter of scale turns out to be critical, and failure to address it properly has prevented a properly grounded understanding of "physical systems", and a proper integration of realist and constructivist worldviews. To illustrate with an example: we use the concept of "object" as short-hand to represent a bounded complex structure that appears distinct from its surroundings. But, the perception of object is scale-dependent. A locked door is an impassable obstacle to a human without the key, but a neutron has a very high probability of passing through undeviated. If the identification of a complex structure as an "object" depends on the scale of observation, this suggests that "objectness" is in the eye of the beholder, not an attribute of the real-world structure: that "objects" are not "real" in physical space-time, but are abstractions, in model-space, of cohesive complex real-world structures. These appear to be "objects" when, and only when, they are observed and perceived at a scale which make their wholeness evident.

(Allen and Starr 2017) and (Aslaksen 2012), arguing from a constructivist position, claim that systems don't exist in the real world, but are only mental constructs that we use to engage with complexity. They advance various arguments in support of this view, notably: that the same "system" can appear completely different when observed at different scales; and that "ontologically, if a system is not a thing, then it doesn't exist". These challenges to the "systems are real" worldview must be properly addressed if systems science is to move towards a properly grounded, unified and ontology sound "realist/constructivist duality", which we believe is desirable. We now discuss how these challenges might be tackled.

The simplest argument in favour of real systems is that, "if observable effects exist that are not attributable to any single 'thing', those effects must be due to interactions between multiple 'things' – therefore, due to 'systems' (Frank, Frank et al. 2016). Such observable effects exist – notably, climate, weather and ecosystem resilience; therefore, 'real' systems exist."

As for the challenge that "if systems exist they must be things" – why? What if the object focus of Western philosophy is simply wrong, or incomplete? Maybe "objects" are mental artefacts, that help us organise and understand our perceptions of the world, as filtered by our brain's (very powerful and highly evolved) subconscious pre-processing. Perhaps we should regard "system" as a distinct form of ontological entity, that can't be shoehorned into a preconceived ontological frame that doesn't allow for Systemness. Perhaps, as Shakespeare said, "There are more things in heaven and earth... than are dreamt of in [our] philosophy".

The preceding paragraphs expose serious issues with the naive realist view of systems. Human brains use abstraction to manage the otherwise overwhelming sensory overload of the observed universe. As our conversation progressed, it seemed that many of the concepts widely taken for granted about real systems are really artefacts of the human brain. These concepts RELATE TO real world observables, but are not THE observables: they are how we have learnt to perceive and interpret nature, and we use them as short-hand to reduce the amount of information we need to process, store and recall. We have already dealt with "object"; the next paragraphs make similar assaults on "boundary" and "pattern".

The concept of "boundary" is a short-hand to describe a discontinuity, or gradient, or impedance to flow, in physical space-time. In many biological and some human-made systems, the boundary is very distinct, and different observers using different criteria will tend to agree where the boundary is. However, most physical and societal systems (for example atoms, solar systems, galaxies and social groups) do not have a containing membrane; they are bound together by attractive forces and information flows; and the binding force-field decays progressively rather than abruptly. In these cases, an observer may designate an arbitrary boundary for the purpose of a particular analysis; but other observers with different purposes are likely to choose different boundaries. And further, in some types of system, one element may be a member of several containing systems simultaneously. This suggests that "belongingness" and the associated "binding processes" may be more fundamental to real systems than "boundaries".

The upshot of this discussion is that while "boundary" is often quoted as a key property of systems, we have to conclude (as the constructivists have argued all along) that a boundary is observer-designated. In many systems it will map to an observable: a gradient or discontinuity in an entropy- or force-field; or a change in density, or in the form of organisation. But the real-world observable is the gradient; the boundary is an abstraction in model-space.

And finally, the concept of "pattern" is an abstraction used to represent recurring relationship structures observed in a complex organisation. So, the observable is the organisational state of the system, while "pattern" is an abstraction in model-space that allows us to condense and summarise the information. Patterns are very important, because, by matching their respective patterns, we can explore similarities and differences between the organisation of different real-world systems. The concept of an "isomorphy", widely discussed in systems science, involves situations where the same formal system is a valid encoding for different "natural" systems. (Francis 2018) describes how Physicists are now using isomorphies to study inaccessible systems, by observing accessible isomorphs or "analogues" of the system of real interest. This is evidence of real synergy between the concepts of modern Physics and those of General Systems Theory.

We can summarise the preceding discussion in the following table.

Real-world observable	Model-space abstraction
Real-world system: observable due to a) Persistent region of low entropy; b) Behaviour not attributable to single "object".	System model
Matter-energy continuum	Discrete Objects
Gradient	Boundary
Organisation, entropy	Pattern

To establish a good scientific foundation for "physical systems", we need to go back to fundamentals to address these insights, and other valid objections to "naïve realism".

There is much debate in the systems community about "the threshold of systemness"- in other words, "what are the minimum criteria for something to be considered a system?" The seven different worldviews identified in the INCOSE surveys (see "worldviews" section of this report) were distinguished largely by the perceived "threshold of and criteria for systemness". If different systemists cannot agree on what is a system, agreement on the nature of the science of systems is likely to elude us.

From a science perspective we would look for observable discriminants between System and non-System, and between different types of system. Our discussions had a number of starting points, perhaps owing to different scientific backgrounds.

INCOSE (2018) suggests that "a more fundamental definition of system would be *a persistent region of low entropy (= high organisation) in physical or conceptual space-time*. Then, it would follow that *systemness is the phenomenon that allows regions of organisation to persist in a dissipative universe*. Physics tells us that the universe is ruled by the second law of thermodynamics, which states that in a closed system, entropy increases over time [1] [2]..

This is perhaps only part of the story. Simple physical system default to a stable equilibrium state with low entropy and low energy. However, an open system can keep its entropy low – i.e. maintain its ordered state - without violating the second law, by using energy from, and thereby increasing the entropy of, its surroundings. This **energy flow** drives the biological processes of auto-organization and emergence - and also complex non-equilibrium physical (non-biological!) systems such as gas turbines, plate tectonics, and stars. The membrane boundary of most living (and many man-made) systems allows a very high entropy gradient, almost a discontinuity, at the system boundary. This creates the conditions for low entropy systems to operate at high levels of energy, far from equilibrium – the conditions for self-sustaining life [3].

Turning towards general systems theory, a general pattern of systemness can be described in the following terms. A system is an organised set of parts with properties of the whole that the parts do not exhibit when acting alone or in a different form of organisation. The parts of the system may themselves be systems **at a lower level of organisation**. Unpacking this in the diagram below,, we can say that, for a system at a given level of organisation:

1.   the parts of the system:

o   are constrained by their membership of the system - (Heylighen 1995) describes a system as "a constraint on variety";

o   in return, get some benefit from membership [4] [5] [6] - a more stable environment, more opportunities, or merely survival;

2.   the more complex structure of the system of interest gives rise **to new degrees of freedom** at the system level, not available to the individual parts of the system;

3.   these additional degrees of freedom give rise to

o   new types of systemic properties (emergent properties), and

o   the potential for new types of relationships, or what (Norman 1990) would call new "affordances for interaction".

IFSR Conversation 2018

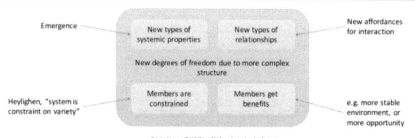

(Volk 2017) and (Smith and Morowitz 2016) demonstrate that some construct of this general form applies recursively at every level of integration **in an unbroken sequence** from atom to planet, and indeed to galaxy. Volk identifies a "grand sequence" of twelve levels of organisational complexity from "quarks to culture". He introduces the term "combogenesis" to describe the potential for creation of higher evolutionary levels by novel combinations at existing ones. Smith and Morowitz show how the basic recursive system pattern (each new level of organisation enabling new types of property and new types of interaction) provides a mechanism rich enough to generate life on an energy- and chemical-rich planet.

We can summarise this part of the argument with four key points:

- Combogenesis sequence: a chain of levels of organisation, capable (under suitable conditions) of generating new higher levels of complex organisation by means of interactions at the existing levels;
- Dependency chains: each level of combogenesis can only happen after certain enablers are in place at the level below;
- Increasing complexity over time WITHIN each level of organisation - e.g. organs appeared as subsystems in multicellular organisms: organs are only viable and only have useful purpose within the context of the multi-cellular organism, so they did not evolve before multi-cellular organisms, they could only develop once the step to multicellular organisms had been made;
- Higher level of combogenesis can be viewed at multiple scales: at a single point in time we observe multiple levels of organisation in any one system.

(Rousseau, Wilby et al. 2018) offer a simplified six-step version of Volk's "Grand Sequence" and add the important side-branch "macro-physical systems":

1. micro-physical systems
2. chemical systems
3. macro-physical systems
4. biological systems
5. social systems
6. socio-technical systems

If we can understand similarities and differences across these major classes of system, we have a clear foundation for a properly founded science of physical (or real, or natural, or concrete...) systems, that spans the existing scientific disciplines and clearly links to conceptual systems and systems thinking through Rosen's Modelling Relation.

Reflections on the nature of engagement with systems
(Swami Natarajan)

- Purposes of engagement and pattern of practice organization
- Worldviews: Six dimensions
- Systemology: The nature of engagement with systems
- 4 worlds: Observing, understanding and modelling systems. The formation of knowledge
- The scientific method: Developing validated knowledge
- Challenges in developing validated models for complex systems
- Knowledge Integration

People engage with systems in the real world for a variety of purposes, including understanding them, discovering their principles of functioning and building models, predicting the behaviour of natural systems and how it might affect their life, engineering new systems, managing existing systems, modifying and transforming systems to better suit their purposes. A large portion of the body of knowledge in systems science, and related fields such as systems engineering, systems thinking and systems transformation, focuses not on studying systems in the real world and building models and theories to explain observable phenomena, but on examining how people engage with systems and the real world to build knowledge, and developing guidance on how we should engage with systems to achieve these purposes. Of course, since people are part of the real world, one could argue that such study is also part of the science! In any case, the discipline of systems science encompasses not only knowledge about the nature of systems, but also the nature of how we engage with systems,

People's engagement with systems can be organized in terms of various areas of systems practice, corresponding to our purposes in engaging with systems: systems understanding; knowledge formation in the form of explanatory and predictive models; integration of knowledge into a consistent discipline, and across disciplines; systems engineering; systems management; systems intervention and transformation. Systems science includes studying systems practice in each of these areas, with the goal of showing how the practice knowledge and guidelines in each of these areas arises naturally from fundamental theories in the discipline about the nature of systems and the nature of our engagement with systems.

As discussed earlier, worldviews play a foundational role in our engagement with systems, since they guide both the focus of our observations and experiences of systems, and our interpretation of these to form knowledge model and practice guidelines. Systems science inquiry into the nature of engagement with systems must begin with the structure of worldviews, their formation and evolution, and their impacts on systems practice. The work on second-order cybernetics (Cybernetics and Von Foerster 1968) ("The observer is part of the system"), the DSRP model that postulates fundamental building blocks that guide our perceptions of systems, and the systemology work referred to above that structures worldviews into six groups of systems are all steps in this direction. A marker of success will be when we have theoretical foundations that enable meaningful dialogue across these worldviews.

Knowledge formation is another key area of inquiry for systems science, particularly because of its potential to influence the formation of systems science knowledge itself. What are the principles that (should) guide the formation of knowledge? The Conversation started our exploration of this area by examining the principles underlying the scientific method, the figure below captures our understanding of this:

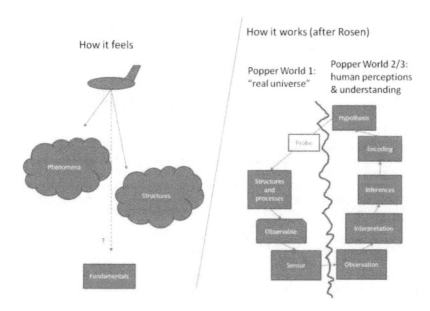

We observe phenomena and structures in the real world, and catch glimpses of the fundamentals that give rise to the observations, but for the most part we have to infer the fundamentals through the systematic process shown on the right (Popper 1979). The key elements of this process are the principles that hypotheses must be testable and tested based on observations of the world of interest, and that we must explicitly design probes and data gathering that facilitate falsification, confirmation or refinement of the hypothesis.

Other principles are more open to debate, particularly in terms of applicability to knowledge formation in more complex systems. Science has been very successful in developing models with excellent explanatory and predictive power for "natural systems": physical systems and living systems. Even for these, as the systems involved get more complex e.g. weather systems, it becomes extremely challenging to build high quality testable models. Applying the scientific method to build knowledge in complex human activity systems e.g. social systems, economic systems, political systems has proven far more difficult.

There are several challenges in applying the method to complex human activity systems:

- The number of variables (potential influencers of phenomena) involved is very large, and it is difficult to even know whether all likely influencers have been included in the model.

- Controlled experimentation is typically not possible.
- There are limits on observability. For example, we can observe a purchasing decision, but not the driving factors that led to the purchase.
- Many of the factors (model variables) may be intrinsically subjective e.g. perceived value.
- Outcomes in these systems often involve complex interplays among factors. With large numbers of variables and complex inter-relationships and interplay, the potential phenomenological space becomes vast, with the result that observations cover only tiny islands within the space that the model must address, particularly in view of limits on controlled experimentation.

These limitations impact other principles that are commonly cited as part of the scientific method: objective data gathering, independent testability, testable predictions.

Extending the scientific method to such complex systems is important not only to knowledge formation in human activity disciplines, but also to developing a systems science that is valid across all types of systems. Distilling the essence of the scientific method to the process depicted and the two key principles indicated earlier might facilitate the design of a knowledge formation approach applicable to complex human activity systems.

Systemology presents a model of knowledge formation and evolution in four interrelated spheres of systems practice: philosophy, science, engineering and realisation (living within society) introduced at the beginning of this report. The model is potentially applicable both at the level of individual disciplines and to systems as a whole, and perhaps even to particular localized contexts of knowledge formation e.g. enterprises, projects. A widely accepted theory of knowledge formation that can guide the practice of knowledge formation across disciplines is a critical need to be addressed by systems science, as part of its inquiry into the nature of engagement with systems.

Knowledge integration is another key area of inquiry. A problem that is widely perceived is that knowledge is increasingly fragmented into disciplines. Interdisciplinary and multidisciplinary efforts create bridges between disciplines on a case-by-case basis but without strong foundations for integration and synergy. Recently, it has been postulated that systems science (and allied fields such as systems engineering) could be a transdiscipline that transcends individual disciplines, and which should create foundational understanding that enables disciplines to come together. The four spheres of practice model points out that many disciplines focus on particular aspects (e.g. chemistry, structural mechanics), while others (e.g. biology) engage with wholes, in which multiple aspects come together, and proposes principles that explain how wholes relate to each other, and to aspects. The concept of ontogenesis (also called combogenesis) examines how new domains arise by combination of elements in already existing domains, resulting in new elements (structures and phenomena) with new degrees of freedom, leading to new classes of behaviour and new fields of study. Systems science is a foundational science ("metascience") that should address this need for transdisciplinary understanding and integration.

Other areas of systems practice, including systems engineering, systems management, systems intervention and systems transformation, have empirically derived bodies of knowledge relating to application of knowledge to address needs and solve problems. Systems science inquiry should indicate how this empirical knowledge follows naturally from application of the fundamental principles of systems science.

The power of frameworks

(Gary Smith)

- Foundational knowledge in chemistry
- Analogous thinking for "systemry"
- Utility for system science of such a framework

When we first start school there are generally three sciences that are first taught as foundations. One of these is chemistry. If you were to ask the question, "what do you know about chemistry" of almost anyone, they would know some of these fundamentals and depending on their level of interest and understanding these would increase in number and richness, can you imagine a future world in which system science is understood in a similar way?

Chemistry	System analogy - Systemry
Every substance is made of atoms	Everything is made of systems
There are different types of atoms known as elements	There are different types of systems and we can refer to these as classes
There is a diagram called the periodic table that shows all the elements in an organised way	There will be a diagram, perhaps called the systemic table that shows all the classes in an organised way
Elements share a foundational structure comprised of protons, neutrons and electrons	Systems share a foundational structure comprised of information, knowledge, forces, mass and energy (or something like this).
Atoms of the same element have the same chemical properties	Systems of the same class have the same systemic properties
The elements can be organised within groups and the elements within these groups share similar properties (i.e. alkali metals)	System classes can be organised within groups and the classes within these groups share similar properties
Elements within a group are organised in increasing levels of electron orbits	Classes within a group are organised in increasing levels of complexity
Elements across groups are organised at the same scale of electron orbits and ordered by atomic number	Classes across groups are organised at the same scale of complexity and ordered by systemic number (we will need to work out what this is and what the implications might be)
Atoms can bond with other atoms to create chemical substances that have very different properties from the atoms comprising the substance	Systems can bond with other Systems to create more complex systems than can have very different properties to the comprising systems
There are two main types of bonds and these types of bonds have an strong influence on the behaviour of the chemical substances	There are two main (likely in actuality a few but not many) types of bonds (physical, informatic) and these types of bonds have an strong influence on the behaviour of the emergent system
There are chemical reactions that take place between elements and substances and these lead to the formation of new substances	There are systemical reactions that take place between classes and things and these lead to the formation of new things
Sometimes chemical reactions produce heat from these reactions and sometimes they take in heat	Sometimes systemical reactions produce heat from these reactions and sometimes they take in heat
There are several branches of chemical knowledge that are distinctly taught but these all are based on foundational concepts and principles	There are several branches of systemic knowledge (systemology) that are distinctly taught but these all are based on foundational concepts and principles
Within this knowledge there is a huge repository of the different types of reactions and the way these reactions can be used in everyday life, in the laboratory and in industry	Within this knowledge there is a huge repository of the different types of reactions and the way these reactions can be used in everyday life, in the laboratory and in industry
The illustration of the elements arranged in the periodic table provides a very powerful tool for understanding properties and relationships even for those elements for which the chemist is less familiar	The illustration of the systemics arranged in the systemic table will provide a very powerful tool for understanding properties and relationships even for those classes for which the systemologist/systemist is less familiar

At first sight, depending on your prevailing worldview you might think this is somewhat adventurous and you would be right, but maybe taking into account Volks grand sequence and Rousseau's six levels of complexity, Troncale's "unbroken sequence of origin" we are not that far away from a workable model.

Perhaps by looking at the six levels of complexity, distinguishing the system classes and organising them by scale we will discover an emergent pattern for systemic number. Knowledge of such a number could have similar utility to that of the atomic number in chemistry for the understanding of systemness. Another intriguing exercise will be to consider the relationship of the isomorphisms across groups and within groups.

Distributed across all of the different branches of systemic practice we have a vast existing knowledge base, imagine if we could find a way of integrating this knowledge with reference to the same framework of foundational concepts and principles. Can you imagine how powerful a tool this would be?

Structuring, using and testing a knowledge framework for system science
(Swami Natarajan)

- Basic structure of a system science knowledge framework
- Tests to determine whether an entry is right
- Consistency relationships within the framework
- Intended uses

Distinct from the Systemic table which considers system 'periodicity' and the organisation of system classes, another potentially useful framework that was developed during the Conversation organizes systems science knowledge. It consists of two tables, one for organizing knowledge about systems, and the other for organizing systems practice knowledge.

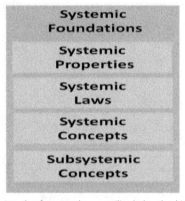

As a source of material for experimentation using the framework, we utilised the the big picture conceptualisation of   system isomorphie prepared by the "Active and Healthy Aging" Linz team.Attempting to place the isomorphies they had used within this simple framework alongside other concepts and theories of systemic knowledge.

Systemic Practice   Systemic Foundations

Small circles are isomophies – evident within the framework as a mixture of concepts

Our intent was not to be exhaustive (or with complete consensus due to time) but to see if existing systems science knowledge could usefully be organised in this sort of structure. We concluded that it could, and that such a structure offers promise in accommodating the wealth of knowledge and viewpoints found in the system science community.

Just as with the periodic table of elements, ideally we would like such a framework to have the following characteristics:

- The structure of the framework should reflect fundamental structures in the discipline.
- It should facilitate not only the capture but the evolution of knowledge in the discipline.
- It should indicate gaps and inconsistencies in current knowledge, and point out areas that need to be explored further to develop new knowledge.
- It should be intuitive and easy for practitioners with different levels of ability and different goals to use. It is to be expected that researchers in the domain might get far more out the framework than casual users.
- It should drive a transformation in both the self-perception and external perception of the field as having evolved from a chaotic collection of disparate knowledge to a coherent discipline.

The framework design would be based on the following principles:

- Each entry in the table captures knowledge related to a particular systems phenomenon or characteristic. The structure of the row represents the systems principle that outcomes arise from elements coming together in a pattern of organization, within some context. Accordingly, each row includes the phenomena or behaviour to be explained, the context of applicability of the knowledge, the elements involved, and the pattern of organization.

- The substructure of patterns of organization reflects the knowledge formation lifecycle (eg. hypothesis, theory, principle, law). Knowledge may be either empirical or theoretical. Empirical knowledge evolves from observations (cases or scenarios) to empirical rules to empirical models that purport to explain the behaviour. Theoretical knowledge progresses from conjectures to theories with an associated confidence level to laws and principles. The position of the entries within this pattern of organization reflects where we are in the knowledge formation life cycle relative to that particular class of phenomena.
- Context of applicability is an interesting attribute, because it reflects worldviews. When knowledge is initially created (not only empirical knowledge, but even theoretical findings) we may not be aware of the frame of validity, and may consider it to be universal. Over time, we may become aware of the frame within which we have been operating, so we be able to identify contextual qualifiers - this indicates worldview expansion and maturation of understanding.
- Ideally, the rows should be ordered to reflect a progression of concepts, so that later rows build on knowledge in the earlier rows. However, we have not managed to introduce such ordering so far. We have examined the possibility of separating phenomena and characteristics applicable to all systems from those applicable only to particular classes of systems or contexts, but grouping rows by context of applicability feels like a usage convenience rather than a fundamental framework design principle. A possible approach is to arrange rows as a progression of explanation, so that advanced phenomena refer to simpler phenomena, and laws, principles and patterns that have been already encountered. More work is needed in this area.
- Each row identifies the vocabulary of elements in terms of which the knowledge is expressed. Ideally we should be able to identify a few "fundamental" elements / concepts, such that all others can be derived from these. This is yet to be done, but the framework provides for this as a goal of the discipline.
- While the framework is intended primarily for capturing systems science knowledge, the same framework can be used for capturing knowledge in other domains as well. This reflects the role of systems science as a transdiscipline or "metascience", that every discipline seeks to explain phenomena in terms of basic concepts, and patterns of organization with associated laws and principles.
- Ideally, the ordering of domains along rows can themselves be arranged so that they reflect the principle of ontogenesis: that elements from one or more domains combine to generate phenomena that are interpreted as structural elements (entities, operations / interactions, properties) at a higher level of organization e.g. the phenomena of physics provide the elements and concepts in chemistry. Organizing disciplines in this way captures the layering of knowledge in disciplines.
- As mentioned earlier, the framework actually consists of two tables. One table captures knowledge about systems (and if desired, knowledge in other disciplines derived from observation of various kinds and aspects of systems). The other table captures knowledge about systems practice i.e. how we engage with systems. In the practice table, instead of phenomena and explanations of phenomena in terms of patterns of organization, the focus is on purposes and knowledge related to purpose accomplishment in terms of patterns of activity. This includes both empirical knowledge such as methods, guidelines and rules of practice, as well as formal knowledge such as techniques, models (e.g. analysis models) and principles that have a

theoretical basis. The methods are expressed in terms of practice concepts, and again, ideally we would like to discover practice fundamentals.

- In this table also, we can restrict ourselves to capturing systems practice knowledge, or we can also use it to capture practice knowledge in other disciplines, such as engineering, management and social systems practice disciplines.

During the Conversation, we developed some tests for deciding whether an entry belonged in a particular column e.g. is it a phenomenon or characteristic, is it a concept of systems, is it a fundamental concept applicable to all systems and so on. We need to extend these criteria to determine whether a particular knowledge item is a conjecture, a theory, a law, a principle etc. - current nomenclature is somewhat haphazard. We understand that there is other work going on in the systems science community addressing this, and we plan to work with them to establish the extended criteria. We are currently in the process of reaching out to the community to socialize the framework and work together to populate it.

Our intention is that the framework should be used in the following way:

- By organizing the knowledge in this way, the systems science community can see how all the systems science knowledge that has been developed over the past several decade relates to each other. Where there are multiple competing models to explain a phenomenon or characteristic, or multiple methods to address particular practice goals, it collates them within a single row, serving as a prelude to examining how they relate to each other e.g. methods and explanations may have differing contexts of applicability, based on their underlying assumptions. If a method, model or explanation only works with particular worldviews, that should be noted as part of the context of applicability. The community should also be able to reason about consistency relationships across rows, based on the principles defined above. Thus the framework should facilitate knowledge integration within the discipline: pulling together all the knowledge into a coherent, consistent discipline with known gaps.

- It makes visible where each knowledge item is in the knowledge formation process, thereby fuelling further research in the field to progress them towards accepted theories, laws and principles. There may be debates about whether an item belongs in a particular column, but the tests should help settle that, or the very existence of a dispute indicates gaps in the field. If there are phenomena for which there is no explanation, or conjectures and theories with no corresponding empirical data and validation, it makes that visible. If there are consistency gaps e.g. explanations for different phenomena are based on incompatible concepts or assumptions, that becomes evident as well.

- Researchers would have a single knowledge base to which they can go both to identify what is known in the area, and to make entries based on the work that they are doing. Practitioners would also have a single knowledge base to which they can go to get pointers on knowledge and practices to achieve their goals. Thus it provides a foundation for a systems science BoK (body of knowledge) project.

- Another intended use is to work out the relationships between various disciplines. The levels of organization / ontogenetic relationship was referred to earlier, but there are also other kinds of relationships among disciplines e.g. that phenomena in one discipline are impacted by concepts from other discipline. The references from concepts in one discipline to concepts in other

We believe that the framework has the potential to satisfy each of the goals identified above, but this needs to be validated by actually populating it with systems science knowledge and using it as envisioned.

Enabling System Science

(Gary Metcalf)

What is the path to create a systematic enterprise for system science?

The proposition that "everything is a system" or alternatively that "everything is comprised of systems" implies that there must be universal characteristics common to all systems. The search for the most general or fundamental characteristics of all systems is essentially the search for a General System Theory, such as proposed by Bertalanffy. That would be the universal model, theoretically uniting not only all sciences, but also philosophy, art, spirituality, etc.

Even entertaining such a notion is difficult. Scientists tend to see reality in terms of a timeline that builds a hierarchy. The Big Bang begat all matter and energy, from which came the particles that turned into atoms which turned into molecules — which eventually became the biosphere and the global human civilizations that we have on Earth today (including all of the ecosystems and species that went before us). If so, then all patterns of organization (types of systems) must also have been formed in that way.

It may also be helpful to remember that the "social sciences" (e.g. economics) are still barely accepted as science, if at all, by many in the natural sciences. If there are universal principles of systems, then they should apply across all domains. One possibility, though, would be that as systems become more complex (e.g. more dynamic, and with greater levels of hierarchy) they exhibit systemic qualities more obviously, and require more systemic understanding. The context for particle physics, for instance, should be the entire universe (assuming that it is as uniform as scientists believe). This environment affected the particles as the universe cooled. Living organisms on the Earth are highly context-dependent, requiring significant stability with respect to temperature and the gaseous contents of the atmosphere. Human cultures have shown significant stability in some cases, but are also highly volatile and sensitive to threats of change perceived in their environments.

As systems science advances, what principles should guide its development? Some proponents argue that it must be "a science," but exactly what that implies is not clear. It might mean that data are empirical and subject to experimental testing. It might mean that descriptions must be mathematical. It might imply that theories are accepted by bodies of leading scientists (i.e. a normative evaluation).

The advancement of systems science might also imply an iterative process through which principles are tested within specific realms, and are adopted when found to be applicable across many domains [7]. Systems biology, for instance, has incorporated a number of principles from both systems science and complexity science, as it expands beyond molecular biology. Some of those might be interpreted or adapted to engineering in order to test their relevance. Engineering itself may already be moving in systemic directions, even if not called such, through movements like evolutionary engineering. Systems engineering, of course, has explicitly adopted systemic principles in concept, but thus far without sufficient foundation as a science for the basis of systems engineering as a distinct discipline.

The future development of systems science will require collaboration between high-level theorists who can identify the most general principles and those working within specific domains who can see the principles and the connections. That collaboration, by itself, would represent a need addressed by early systems scientists. It is also a challenge, give the highly specialized nature of funding and support for research. The work of this conversation team has represented one way of advancing systems science [8].

We have been experimenting with the Kumu tool a way to identify the interfaces between systems people, work products, initiatives and organisations. We were wondering if this might be something that could be used to flow and help develop systems science utilising a common framework. Perhaps we might be able to utilise the viable systems model as an overlay on this. Could we create the systematic enterprise that we require for systems science in this way?

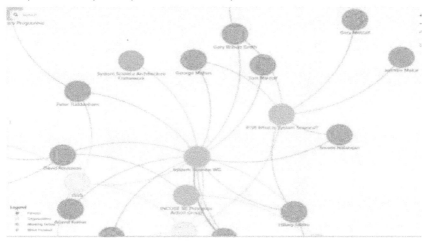

https://embed.kumu.io/15c0df2fd2397616a62f5354fd4f78dd

Reflections on the experience and conclusions
Jennifer Makar / Gary Smith

When we look back at the journey we took, we started out with a feeling, a hope that something might be possible to clear the clouds and blinkers (resultant from different worldviews, experiences and backgrounds) that would allow diverse systems people to see that actually they did share or were able to derive shared foundations through conversation. It was hoped that through this conversation we might be able to then share and communicate these foundations across the systems community and through this start to create a systematic enterprise for systems science. To be able to begin the task of integrating collectively our systems knowledge within a framework.

As we continue to share ideas and concepts for system science, certain key diagrams or viewpoints are emerging. A draft of this IFSR report formed the basis of a two day extended conversation between Patrick Godfrey, James Martin, David Rousseau, Gary Smith, Hillary Sillitto and Michael Wilkinson at which the diagram below was sketched. Population of these viewpoints with our knowledge of system science will we believe facilitate a convergence of people and practice. Early exposure and utilisation of these viewpoints has already identified additional opportunities.

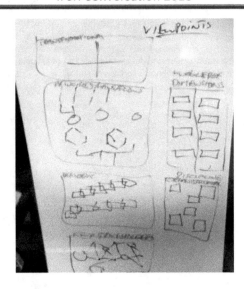

It is envisaged that through key viewpoints like these and perhaps a few others, such as a capability viewpoint for system science that we might be able to integrate our knowledge. All of these viewpoints making reference to a foundational data structure.

Through the conversation we identified that the essence of systems be they conceptual or physical is that systems could be organised. We are hopeful that with system science we can better understand how to create, transform, maintain, evolve systems that are useful for humankind in harmony. An organised systematic enterprise for systems science is our vision, one that we hope you might be able to share.

Allen, T. F. and T. B. Starr (2017). Hierarchy: perspectives for ecological complexity, University of Chicago Press.

Aslaksen, E. W. (2012). The system concept and its application to engineering, Springer Science & Business Media.

Cabrera, D. and L. Colosi (2008). "Distinctions, systems, relationships, and perspectives (DSRP): A theory of thinking and of things." Evaluation and Program Planning 31(3): 311-316.

Cybernetics, A. S. f. and H. Von Foerster (1968). Purposive systems. Proceedings of the first annual symposium of the American Society for Cybernetics. Edited by Heinz von Foerster [and others], Spartan Books.

Francis, M. R. (2018). "Studying impossible systems with analogues." Physicsworld.

Frank, M., M. Frank, et al. (2016). Systems thinking: Foundation, uses and challenges, Nova Science Publishers, Inc.

Friendshuh, L. and L. Troncale (2012). Identifying fundamental systems processes for a general theory of systems. Proceedings of the 56th Annual Conference, International Society for the Systems Sciences (ISSS), San Jose State University, San Jose, CA, USA.

Gauch Jr, H. G. (2012). Scientific method in brief, Cambridge University Press.

Heylighen, F. (1995). "(Meta) systems as constraints on variation—a classification and natural history of metasystem transitions." World Futures: Journal of General Evolution **45**(1-4): 59-85.

Miller, J. G. (1978). Living systems. Montréal, McGraw-Hill.

Mobus, G. E. and M. C. Kalton (2015). Principles of systems science, Springer.

Morowitz, H. J. (2002). The Emergence of Everything: How the World Became Complex, Oxford University Press.

Norman, D. A. (1990). "The psychology of everyday actions." The Design of Everyday Things. New York: Doubleday/Currency.

Popper, K. (1979). Three worlds, Ann Arbor,: University of Michigan.

Rosen, R. (2012). In J. Rosen, JJ Klineman, & M. Nadin (EDs.), Anticipatory systems: Philosophical, mathematical, and methodological foundations, New York: Springer.

Rousseau, D. and J. Billingham (2018). "A Systematic Framework for Exploring Worldviews and Its Generalization as a Multi-Purpose Inquiry Framework." Systems **6**(3): 27.

Rousseau, D., J. Wilby, et al. (2018). General Systemology: Transdisciplinarity for Discovery, Insight and Innovation, Springer.

Sillitto, H., R. Griego, et al. (2018). What do we mean by "system"?–System Beliefs and Worldviews in the INCOSE Community. INCOSE International Symposium, Wiley Online Library.

Smith, E. and H. J. Morowitz (2016). The origin and nature of life on Earth: the emergence of the fourth geosphere, Cambridge University Press.

Snowden, D. (2000). "Cynefin: a sense of time and space, the social ecology of knowledge management."

Troncale, L. (2013). Systems processes and pathologies: Creating an integrated framework for systems science. INCOSE International Symposium, Wiley Online Library.

Troncale, L. R. (1978). Linkage propositions between fifty principal systems concepts. Applied general systems research, Springer: 29-52.

Volk, T. (2017). Quarks to culture: how we came to be, Columbia University Press.

Von Bertalanffy, L. (1968). "General system theory." New York **41973**(1968): 40.

Waldrop, M. M. (2008). Complexity : the emerging science at the edge of order and chaos. New York, Simon & Schuster Paperbacks.

Team 3 - Active and Healthy Aging

Pamela Buckle (USA /CA)

Gerhard Chroust (AT) [co-leader]

Allenna Leonard (CA)

Shankar Sankaran (AU) [co-leader]

Jennifer Wilby (UK)

The starting point / Motivation

In every part of the world except Africa, the global median age is rising (https://www.visualcapitalist.com/mapped-the-median-age-of-every-continent/). Demographic changes, especially in the developed world, make aging one of today's growing concerns that has far reaching implications. The aim of the Active and Healthy Aging (AHA) program established by the European Union is to foster active and healthy Aging (AHA) among older people in European countries in a sustainable society. Support through AHA's activities has to compensate for more or less insufficient capabilities of Seniors. This is a highly interdisciplinary challenge which involves practically all domains of life: physiology, medicine, psychology, social sciences, society, technology, logistics, infrastructure, architecture, economy, etc.

Worldwide the number of people in the age of over 65 will rise to 1.5 Billion by 2050 (He, 2015), those over 80 will quadruple to 395 million (WHO, 2012). More people than ever before will live beyond 100 years of age. With an increase in the number of people living into advanced old age the incidences of dementia will increase. An estimated 332,000 people were living with dementia in Australia in 2014, of whom 93% are aged 65 and over. The respective number for Austria in 2012 is 145.400 with around 138.000 over 65. In (WHO, 2012) the data all European countries can be found. The number of people with dementia in Australia is estimated to reach almost 900,000 by 2050 and 131.5 million world-wide (AIHW, 2014). The increased prevalence of dementia will impose a substantial economic burden on individuals, the national healthcare system, and the economy at large. Current data shows that total direct healthcare expenditures on dementia is at least $4.9 billion (Dementia-Australia, 2014; AIHW, 2012), and it is expected to account for 11% of the total healthcare expenditure in the world by 2060.

While research is being carried out in relation to how clinical and medical health can be supported through changes to the environment and use of technologies, further research is needed to find other ways to improve quality of life and support general health and well-being including day-to-day activities.

IFSR Conversation 2018

Starting the Conversation Team

ISSS 2017 – workshop

At the 61st ISSS Meeting (Vienna, 2017, (Sankaran, 2017) a workshop was held by Gerhard Chroust and Shankar Sankaran to discuss how systems scientists and thinkers can help to strengthen the resilience of ageing societies. The reason behind this call was the realization that Europe and several developed nations across the world are ageing, due to higher life expectancy, accompanied by a decreasing birth rate. It was estimated that in 2060, 30% of the population in the EU would be older than 65 years. Human worry, suffering, financial problems and grief caused by old age would become a concern for everybody - both the elderly and their families on who they rely for support, This needs increased attention because the physical and mental health of a growing number of persons is seemingly affected reducing their capacity to carry out daily activities Strengthening the resilience of seniors was recognized as necessary but posed a complex interdisciplinary challenge. The question raised at the workshop was 'Can we do a better job of anticipating, understanding systemically, and mitigating the consequences of ageing?' There was a lively discussion and it was suggested that the issue of systemic issues arising for ageing affecting several countries in the world (especially developing countries) could be identified as a potential topic for IFSR Conversation in 2018.

Initiating the Conversation Team 2018

For the IFSR Conversation 2018 (Linz) a call for topics was issued in early 2017 including a proposed topic title 'Active Healthy Aging' (Sankaran, 2017). The Call for Topics had an excellent response, and after intensive discussions by the IFSR Executive Committee 4 topics were chosen for the Conversation, with the topic " Active and Healthy Aging (AHA)" being one of them.

The announcement the topci AHA read as follows:

Demographic changes especially in the Developed World make aging one of today's growing concerns. The aim is to foster Active and Healthy Aging (AHA) in a sustainable society. Support for AHA has to compensate for more or less insufficient capabilities of Seniors. This is a highly interdisciplinary challenge which involves practically all domains of life: physiology, medicine, psychology, social sciences, society, technology, logistics, infrastructure, architecture, economy, etc.

How We Came Together & Aged Together This Week

The Conversation Team

We had several candidates for participation, however, some of them had to cancel in the last minutes due to other pressing obligations, especially due to timing constraint because of the start of the university semester . We especially missed somebody from a Scandinavian country (e.g. Sweden), where a comprehensive and strong health care for aging persons exists.

Five systems researchers finally joined the conversation held between 8th to 13th April , 20018 at St. Magdalena in Linz. They brought a variety of views related to an ageing society from across the world under a topic titled 'Active and Healthy Aging (AHA)', see Appendix A for further details on the team:

- Pamela Buckle (USA/ CA)
- Gerhard Chroust (AT) [co-leader]
- Allenna Leonard (CA)

- Shankar Sankaran (AU) [co-leader]
- Jennifer Wilby (UK)

Kick-off

The team met on the first day of the conversation and started to put down some ideas on what would be their contribution to the conversations? The following overarching question was used to collect ideas:

What do systems theories have to offer people interested in Active Healthy Ageing?

It was acknowledged that the categories of 'aging' and 'aged' incorporated a great deal of variety; dealing with people aged from sixty-five to one hundred and five and with a range of health and economic conditions ranging from healthy to profoundly disabled and from financially secure to destitute (see App. A .2 for the results).

The following key points were captured:

- Scale: impacts on individuals, families, communities, industries, national economies
- Boundary/environmental complexities
- Viable Systems Model (diagnosis of issues, pointing toward design possibilities)
- Homeostats affecting aging populations
- Systemic isomorphies (pertaining to various clusters)
- Causal loop diagrams
- Case study
- Psychological understanding
- Process knowledge
- Tools and concepts supporting research into aging.

Approaches

The AHA team initially discussed two possible approaches to gather all the concerns of the members of the team related to ageing: drawing of rich pictures (Soft Systems Methodology (Checkland, 2009) and brain storming. Brainstorming was finally selected as the approach and 101 issues were gathered and clustered under the following nine broad themes:

1. Culture and Social Norms (Integration, Separation ...)

2. Transiting (what age is 'aged'?) and for what purpose are the categories designed

3. Risk and Opportunity (vulnerability, time for volunteering)

4. Loss & Resilience (loss of hearing, memory ,,,)

5. Internal - External (meaning of life, society..,)

6. Caring Relationships (family and friends, intergenerational groups)

7. Assisted Living (renovations, tools, home-help, seniors' home ...)

8. Degree of Autonomy (ability to choose, ...)

9. Governance and Policy (models of care, finances, etc.)

We also used System Isomorphises (systems theorists seek out isomorphism in systems so to create a synergetic understanding of the intrinsic behaviour of systems, see https://en.wikibooks.org/wiki/Systems_Theory/Isomorphic_Systems).

We used it as another lens to categorize the issues (a set of properties associated with a system) by mapping our ideas into a generic system:

1. Hierarchy and Complexity (Structure/Form)

2. Mechanisms of the system (Systems flow and processes)

3. Information (Information flows)

4. Defining the system (Boundary)

5. Maintenance and viability of the system (System maintenance)

6. Response to disturbances (System evolution)

A result of this analysis is shown in Figure 1.

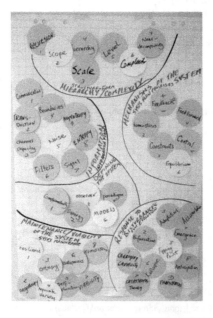

Figure 1 : Isomorphic representation of issues associated with AHA.

Adopting a VSM-Model

Allenna Leonard suggested using Viable System Modelling (VSM) as way of analysing issues associated with Active Healthy Aging.

What is a VSM-Model?

A Viable System Model (VSM) is a 5-level model of the organizational structure of any autonomous system. A viable system is any system organized in such a way as to meet the demands of surviving in the changing environment. VSM was developed by Stafford Beer who acknowledged the influence of Ross Ashby and Warren McCulloch.

One of the prime features of systems that survive is that they are adaptable. The VSM encompasses five management functions that any viable system must have: activities that bring reward from the present environment, means of coordinating those activities, a decision making function regarding the present situation, an audit function to take occasional measures of relevant issues, a means of addressing the near, mid and long term future and an identity/coherence function that guides the choices among alternatives that are available.

The Wilma-Scenario – a VSM Model

It was decided to use VSM model for a typical person who is aging. An "aging person living in a town in Austria" was proposed. Gerhard helped in developing a profile of Wilma and all team members added to the profile to build a realistic and comprehensive profile of a typical ageing person in a developed country. We characterized her as retired teacher, Christian faith, a grandmother, a widow, active as volunteer in social activities, having diabetic and arthritic problems.

Figure 2 : Wilma (courtesy: https://www.storyblocks.com/images/elderly)

As a preparation for an analysis using VSM isomorphism were used to discuss the Wilma System including: how we can define the system, identify information issues; explore maintenance/viability of the system; mechanisms of the system; responses to disturbance; and hierarchy/complexity. Interestingly, during the discussion, considerable differences between different countries (especially USA, Canada, Austria and Sweden) were detected, especially with respect to health service.

The following questions were arrived at as key decisions to be made by Wilma and/or her environment that will result in a holistic plan for her life:

1. Where will I live?
2. What is my relationship to my family?
3. Who are my friends/companions?
4. How will I occupy myself?
5. What services do/will I need?
6. What will I do for fun?

7. How will I live a full life?

8. How will I pay for it all?

9. Have I got an 'end of life' plan?

10. What will be my legacy?

Applying the Viable Systems Model

The VSM analysis of Wilma resulted is trying to understand what a typical ageing person should consider enjoying an active and healthy life.

The following five levels of VSM were then used to analyse the Wilma system:

Level 5 (Identity and coherence)

Level 4 (Anticipating the future environment)

Level 3 (Managing the here and now)

Level 3* (Periodic audit)

Level 2 (Coordination)

Level 1 (Operations connected to the present environment)

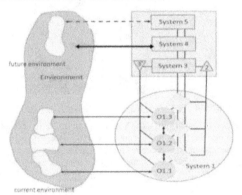

Level 5 (Identity & Coherence) :

- Lives in a smaller village in Austria
- Retired teacher
- Christian faith
- Grandmother
- Widow
- Volunteer in social activities
- Currently well balanced
- Diabetic and Arthritic problems

Level 4 (Anticipating the Future Environment):

IFSR Conversation 2018

POSITIVE

- Opportunities to travel
- Freedom from obligations and unwanted tasks
- ability to spend time and money as she wishes
- thinks of taking up new courses or hobbies

NEGATIVE

- Emerging health issues
- uncertainty concern : diabetes, arthritis
- Evolving diabetic treatment
- Increased mobility issues
- Social relations (?)
- Anticipation of loneliness
- Maintaining friends (?)
- Friends dying recently
- Grandchildren growing up
- Concerns about safety/security
- Uncertainty about staying in her house
- Legacy reflections

Level 3 (Managing the Here and Now):

- Managing house with help
- Managing budget (now)
- Coping with stairs
- Driving (only in daylight)
- Insurance/Tax (Managing)
- Giving/Receiving Services
- Examples of Audit Practice
- Visits to doctor
- Children visiting here, noticing changes
- Priest checking up
- Insurance- House inspection
- Neighborhood check in
- Buddy system

Level 2 - Coordination

- Calendar
- television
- computer and internet connections and security
- Bills
- Coordinating transport
- Mobility (Physical/Exercise)
- Security - Locks/Keys
- Medical visits
- Monitor medical side effects
- Pill schedules
- How to locate and use services

Level 1 - Operations Connected to the Environment

Mechanisms of the System

- Hierarchy/Complexity
- Feedback: ongoing efficacy of her medication must be monitored and communicated between her and her health care providers
- Response to Disturbance
- Tipping Point: event such as a fall could change her life drastically
- Values her small town
- External services (economy: only those services required by a substantive number of people in her community will be available to Wilma)
- Shrinking choices/options
- Vulnerability to crime

Activities

- More discretionary time
- House/Garden care, Maintenance (Fun)
- Self Maintenance: Health, relations, dignity, hobbies
- Legal, Financial
- Voluntarism; library; church

Personal Connections

- Caring, Family relationship plus links
- Friends
- Neighborhood
- Public services
- Connectivity through phone, text, social media, etc.
- Internet Info – Networks – Media

Algedonic Signals

The team also considered algedonic signal (signals that can cause major perturbation to a system) which could affect the Wilma System's Viability. Algedonics 'is the scientific study of pleasure and pain' <https://en.wiktionary.org/wiki/algedonics>.

The algedonic signals that could have a significant effect on the viability of the Wilma systems were identified as:

- Injury
- Financial windfall
- Severe illness
- Car accident
- Losing important things
- Meeting a new friend or reconnecting with an old friend

Homeostats

Following the analysis using VSM the team explored some homeostats linked to and observed in the Wilma systems. Stafford Beer' approach asks us to look at relationships that are dynamic in a VSM . Ross Ashby showed that only a few simple decision rules in a model could lead to complex interactions.

Often, they are concerned with the maintenance of equilibria called homeostasis with the 'mechanisms' referred to as homeostats (From Allenna Leonard: The First Stafford Beer Memorial Lecture July 8, 2007: The Viable System Model and its Application to Complex Organizations). The homeostats associated with the Wilma System were identified as shown in the Figure below .

Everyone's lives reflect the operation of homeostats whether they are consciously recognized or not; for example, work/life balance, budgeting beyond bare necessities and maintaining physical fitness.

Cost of services - trade off with variety of services
For Wilma, she must make choices around the allocation of her financial resources to the different services she might need or want. These could change over time as better, more accessible or less costly services become available or if she should require more or more expensive services on a temporary or permanent basis.

Internal versus external contacs and support
The internal/external homeostat refers to the balance between her internal life (spiritual, psychological or exploratory) and her external life with family, friends, acquaintances and service providers.

Being ill – being well
The well/ill homeostat refers to activities and choices that keep her well (nutrition, exercise, social and itellectual stimulation) and those that she must recover from as she recovers.

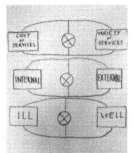

Wilma's homeostats

Final Discussion

Further observations

Gerhard observed the great difference between USA and Austria, which is due to a much better and comprehensive health care system in Austria. In Austria it covers most cost of treatment, even very expensive one. This guarantees a much safer and more reliable outlook to old age.

Gerhard pointed to the Swedish Health care system which is largely tax-funded. It is a system that ensures everyone has equal access to healthcare services. Challenges include funding, quality and efficiency. Even in sparsely populated areas the health care system is fully implemented (see https://www.weforum.org/agenda/2019/01/what-can-america-learn-from-sweden-about-healthcare/)

Pamela noted that aging represents not just a diminishment of a person's capacities, but can also be considered an important developmental stage in adult life, with unique psychological strengths and the potential for vibrant new experiences as well.

Conclusions

The team concluded that using Wilma' profile as an example helped to make the discussions to come close to reality. Further observations from the team were:

1. VSM is an appropriate framework to investigate the issue of healthy ageing

2. System biology is an important aspect of ageing we also need to consider.

3. Examples of how simple systems set up by themselves in the community can be effective support without relying on external help (Allenna Leonard)

4. Legal aspects of healthcare (how different countries view this aspect of society?). This may need further exploration.

5. Provide volunteering opportunities for the aged to give more meaning to their life.

6. While technology can help there are barriers in adoption

Our process - how we worked together:

The team had very enjoyable and productive discussions weaving together its professional expertise, bringing experiences from various cultures, sharing own experiences, fears and hopes, about aging from personal experiences as well as experiences of loved ones and friends. This resulted in an enjoyable as well as compelling conversation.

The team described their process of working together as

- sharing our professional expertise as systems theorists,
- bringing the perspective of various cultures to the discussion,
- sharing very personal experiences, e.g. our own fears and hopes about aging, from the experiences of our loved ones, and ourselves.
- making conversation interesting and compelling.

The team also discussed how their shared perspectives can be a basis for further work in active and healthy aging.

Some of the ideas were:

- Apply for funding grants
- Potential topics for articles in journals
- Consultation
- Presentations
- Advocacy
  A causal loop diagram (using System Dynamics) was then constructed to identify opportunities for applying for research grants.

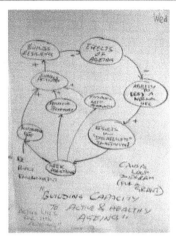

Figure 4: Causal Loop Diagram for research topics and grants

And where we should go from here

Follow up meetings & Dissemination

The conversations ended with a discussion on what the team, along with other systems researchers, could do further to continue addressing systemic aging. The following activities were identified to have potential for further collaboration:

1. Designing interdisciplinary research projects
2. Applying for research grants
3. Writing articles and opinion pieces
4. Exploring consulting opportunities
5. Making presentations
6. Design of interdisciplinary research projects (i.e. the built environment as it relates to notions of 'assisted living')

- A follow up workshop was planned and held at the 62nd ISSS Meeting 2018 at Corvallis, Portland in 2018 which was also completed and a community of inquiry into aging has been set up. (Sankaran, 2018)
- At IDIMT 2018 (interdisciiplinary Information Management Talks) on Serpt 5-7, 2018, in , Kutna Hora, Czech Republic, one session was devoted to e-Health. Topics were e-Health Policies as shown in Active-Healthy Aging (AHA) and Ambient Assisted Living (AAL), (Aumayer-18a).

IFSR Conversation 2018

What did we take away?

Pamela Buckle

Pamela learned much about VSM modelling and about the experiences of the elderly in the various countries of members of our conversation group. With the continued rise in median age, more people than ever before are actively contributing to the workforce, government, and community life. How they are viewed, and view themselves, are interesting dynamics for future research. Pamela was surprised at how readily the conversation oriented and reoriented itself around the struggles and suffering associated with aging, and how difficult it was for the group (herself included) to balance tensions between our understandable concerns about aging with an understanding that older age can also provide opportunities for growth and positive experiences not possible at earlier stages of life.

Gerhard Chroust

Gerhard was surprised and even shocked of the effects of missing uniform and comprehensive health care in the USA, especially with respect to aging, if compared to Austria , Canada and Sweden (and several other European countries).

He welcomed the really interesting way to apply the VSM modelling and he got a profound understanding of the power of the approach.

For his own future life, he recognized and noted things he should do with respect to aging.

Allenna Leonard

Allenna gained a broader appreciation of how systems concepts illuminate the multiple interconnected factors that influence aging and how many of the services and accommodations recommended for aging populations work and improve lives for everyone. A recent cartoon illustrated that point perfectly: only mobile people can easily use stairs but everyone can use a ramp whether they are in a wheelchair or pushing a carriage. It was also energising to collaborate with like-minded people of goodwill who could share their varying perspectives and to become better acquainted with some different methodologies.

Shankar Sankaran

Shankar learnt a lot about how to apply VSM to a living system. He usually uses VSM for organizational analysis and was pleasantly surprised how it helped to use a VSM model of the Wilma system. The broad issues of ageing that may have an impact on the economic and social support systems of developing countries became evident during the conversations revealing the systemic nature of the aging crisis.

References

AIHW *Australia's health 2014,* Austrian Institute of Health and Welfare , Cat. no AUS 178, 2014, pp. 576,

AIHW: AUSTRALIAN INSTITUTE OF HEALTH and WELFARE *Australia's Health, The thirteenth biennial health report* Techn. Report , Australian Institute of Health and Welfare , Cat. no AUS 178, 2012 2012, pp. 642.

AIHW: AUSTRALIAN INSTITUTE OF HEALTH and WELFARE *Australia's health 2014* Techn. Report , Australian Institute of Health and Welfare , Cat. no AUS 178, 2014, pp. 576.

AUMAYR, G. *E-Health Policies in AHA and AAL Projects* in: Doucek, P. , G. CHROUST , V. OSKRDAL, (eds.): *IDIMT-2015, Information Technology and Society - Interaction and Interdependence*, pp. 423–430, Trauner Verlag Linz, Sept. 2018.

BEER, S. *Diagnosing the System for Organizations*. Chichester, John Wiley & Sons, 1985,

BOSI, I., C. COGERINO , B. M. *Real-Time Monitoring of Heart Rate by Processing of Near Infrared Generated Streams* in: *Smart Interfaces 2017, The Sixth International Conference on Smart Systems, Devices and Technologies,* pp. paper 48002, 6 pages IARIA, Italy 2017.

CHECKLAND . P. *Systems Thinking, Systems Practice.* Wiley, Chichester, New York 2009.

CHROUST G. (2017). *Software-basierte Prozessunterstützung für lebenswertes Altern.* In Volland, A., Engstler, M., Fazal-Baqaie, M., E., H., Linssen, O., and M., M., editors, Projektmanagement und Vorgehensmodelle 2017 (PVM-2017), pages 199–206. Gesellschaft f. Informatik, Lecture Notes in Informatics, Vol. P-276, 2017.

CHROUST, G. and AUMAYR, G. (2017). *Supporting active and healthy aging - an assistive process improvement approach.* In Berntzen, L. and Aumayr, G., editors, Smart Interfaces 2017, The Sixth International Conference on Smart Systems, Devices and Technologies, pages paper 48003, 6 pages. IARIA, Italy 2017.

CHROUST, G. and AUMAYR , G. (2018). *Applying process view to active and healthy aging (AHA) problems.* In Rousseau, D., editor, Innovation and Optimization in Nature and Design (Abstracts), pages 72–72, no. 3433. Oregon State University, Corvallis, 2018.

CHROUST, G. and SANKARAN, S., *Team 3: Active and Healthy Aging,* IFSR Newsletter, vol. 35, No 1 (October 2018) pp. 23-24

DEMENTIA AUSTRALIA, *The World Alzheimer's Report 2014* Techn. Report , Dementia Australia, 2014, pp. 104.

EDSON, C.E., BUCKLE, P. H, . SAKARAN S.: A *Guide to Systems Research: Philosophy, Processes, Practice , Philosophy, Processes, Practice ,* Springer 2017

HE, W., D. GOODKIND , P. KOWAL An Aging World: 2015 - International Population Reports Techn. Report , US Census Bureau (census.gov) 2015.

KIRKPATRICK, K. *Sensors for Seniors* Comm. ACM vol. 57 (2014), no. 12, pp. 17–19.

SANKARAN, S. and CHROUST, G. (2017). *Strengthening the resilience of aging societies* (abstract). In Bosch, O., editor, From Science to Systemic Solutions: Systems Thinking for Everyone, pages 109–110. Technical University Wien 2017.

SANKARAN, S. and CHROUST, G. (2018). *Active and healthy aging workshop. In* Rousseau, D., editor, Innovation and Optimization in Nature and Design (Abstracts), pages 91–91, no. 3281. Oregon State University, Corvallis, 2018.

SARFRAZ, M. S., CONSTANTINESCU, A., ZUZEJ, M. , STIEFELHAGEN, R. A *Multimodal Assistive System for Helping Visually Imparied in Social interaction* Informatik-Spektrum vol. 40 (2017), no 6, pp. 540–545.

UNIV. TORINO *My-AHA - My Active and Healthy Ageing* http://www.activeageing.unito.it/home, [retrieved: May, 2017].

WHO: WORLD HEALTH ORGANISATION: *World health day: Are you ready? What you need to know about aging.*
https://www.who.int/world-health-day/2012/toolkit/background/en/, 2012.

Appendix A: Background of Participants

Pamela Buckle (USA/CA)

Pamela Buckle is an Associate Professor of Management at the Robert B. Willumstad School of Business at Adelphi University, New York. and a Visiting Fellow at the University of Bristol's Systems Centre, UK,

Pamela's scholarly and clinical work is oriented around the perspective that human psychology is a complex system embedded in densely-interconnected biological, interpersonal, institutional, and environmental systems. She collaborates with international researchers investigating the cognitive and emotional processes involved in systems thinking, and the worldviews and values systems of systems thinkers. Her interests include the processes involved in scientists' systems thinking, personality structures of systems thinkers, as well as "lay epistemics" (perceptual processes used by nonscientists).

Gerhard Chroust (AT)

Gerhard Chroust is an Austrian systems scientist and Professor Emeritus for Systems Engineering and Automation at the Johannes Kepler University of Linz, Austria. From 1966 to 1991 Chroust worked at the IBM Laboratory Vienna, from 1992 until 2007 he was tenured Professor in Linz. He is a specialist in formal definition of software development processes. He worked in the last years on the impacts of human behaviour and cultural differences on system development. Since 2007 he also performs research on disaster management and in the last few years on issues of human aging, especially in view of supporting humans by information technologies. Since 2017 he took part in the Europe-wide Project ,my-AHA' focused on reduce frailty of older citizens by computer-supported health monitoring and disease prevention.

Allenna Leonard (CA)

Allenna is an American/Canadian consultant in organizational cybernetics based in Toronto. She is a licensee of Team Syntegrity, a director of the Cwarel Isaf Institute and vice-chair of the Ecologos Environmental Institute. Beginning in the 1980's and continuing until his death, she worked with Stafford Beer on a variety of consulting and educational projects, the most prominent being Projecto Urucib in Montevideo Uruguay for the UNDP. Her interests include accountability measures for soft information and applications of cybernetics to governance and ecology. She has taught university courses and published numerous papers and articles. Much of her work is on the use of Beer's Viable System Model and Team Syntegrity Process. She is a past president of the American Society for Cybernetics, and received its McCulloch Award and of the International Society for Systems Science.

Shankar Sankaran (AU)

Shankar Sankaran is a Professor of Organizational Project Management at the School of the Built Environment at the University of technology Sydney in Australia. He is also the President Elect of the International Society of the Systems Sciences in 2018-19. He teaches Systems Thinking to Managers in a Masters program at his university.

Shankar is a member of a research cluster on Healthy Ageing at the Built Environment Informatics and Innovation Centre at his university. He is currently involved in a proposal being submitted to the Australian Government to establish a Cooperative Research Centre for Agile Aging.

Shankar has also been active in promoting Healthy Active Aging as an area of concern at the International Society for the Systems Sciences through facilitating workshop and making presentations at SIG sessions.

IFSR Conversation 2018

Jennifer Wilby (UK)

Jennifer M. Wilby is an American and UK management scientist, and past Director of the Centre for Systems Studies, and a senior lecturer and researcher in management systems and sciences in The Business School, University of *Hull*.

Wilby's research interests is general systems theory, critical system theory and practice. This research include the "systematic and critical review of systems methodologies; hierarchies in organisations; and the use of general system theory and critical systems theory in informing the development of international health policies that reflect both hard (technical) and soft (social) elements in a problem situation".

Appendix B Results of Brainstorming on Monday, April 9. 2018

We collected lists of potential topics for our Conversation

Loss and Resilience :
- Role of loss/reactions to loss
- Loss of ability
- Loss of memory for current retrieval
- Hearing loss
- •• Early onset Alzheimer's-how to handle?
- Mental fitness, Dementia
- – How to measure
- – How to train
- How long will I live?
- 'Out of order!'

Transitioning :
- Aging in different cultures (Hofstede's cultural distinction)
- What age is aged? (boundaries, bifurcation points)
- Physical change / movement
- Shifting social roles
- What are the similarities/differences in adaptive challenges before and during older life?
- Demography
- Lack of tolerance to diminished capacities
- Over-running responsibilities
- Balancing mind and physical ability

Culture and Societal Norms :
- What value-systems are prevalent/useful in early life vs. older life?
- Integration/segregation of people as they age
- Stereotypes of elderly being 50 years (or more) out of date
- Aging in place of living
- 'School dinners'-food options are not ok for different people
- How can old people find a place for their stuff when nobody wants it?
- Are baby boomers different?

Risks and Opportunities :
- Volunteerism opportunities in retirement
- Help for aging parents of disabled disabled children
- Bulling/elder abuse
- Vulnerability to fraud and theft
- Transport and mobility Neurophysiology research
- More vulnerability to effects of climate change (and associated crises)
- Transport and mobility

Assisted Living :
- Tools like a ·courteous intuitive butler'
- Internet-of-things- can help. How?
- Technical (ICT) support- who is in control?
- HCI - Human Computer Interface for seniors
- Digital divide
- Co-housing (especially women growing older)
- What are the unintended consequences of home mediations? (e.g. problem gambling
- Transport and mobility
- If a transport system works for older people, people with carriages. etc. it works for everyone
- Better/clearer traffic signaling
- Day care for elderly. for safety and companionship
- Role of institutions
- Teaching people how to fall (see Netherlands)

Internal and External :
- What kind of life is worth living in older age?
- What provides meaning to life?
- What life activities and experiences can only happen in later life (generative emergence)
- Motivation
- Boredom
- Time - not enough
- Bullying
- Need multiple perspectives on community services for aging (and others)
- Seniors and Maslow's hierarchy of needs : (physiology, safety/security, love/belonging, respect/esteem, self-actualization)

Caring Relationship :
- Family separated by distance (large distance, different country, overseas, estrangement)
- The role of grandparents in society
- 3-generation (or 5-generation) housing
- Role of family and friends

- Role of families/surrogate families
- Inter-generational support
- Peer support

Governance (and Policy) :
- Role of institutions
- What boundaries are appropriate as people age? (financial decisions)

- Transport and mobility Personal decisions
- Discrimination
- Not political control over 'big' decisions or money
- Legislative protection of pension rights Cost of medication/medical care

- Transport and mobility

- Quality assurance from measurement to advice? ISO standards
- Death-planning, death industries
- Real time monitoring of health/well being vs. privacy
- Politics of aging care
- Financial issues
- Results of income inequality
- Many accommodations are unaffordable
- Role of pharmaceutical companies (and their profit maximization)
- Legal issues
- Nursing home staff under-paid

Degrees of Autonomy :
- Keeping Fitness
- Moving/ changing interest
- Social integration
- Who decides when sex, alcohol, marijuana is not ok?
- What happens when older people are still able to contribute significantly?
- Compassion in small cities
- Where do I live when I grow old?
- Living dead via technology aimed at longevity
- Accessibility to health care
- Deciding on retirement
- Ability to choose (e.g. meals, etc.)

TEAM 4: Data Driven Systems Engineering: An MBE Manifesto

Edward R. Carroll (US) [Team Leader]
Dana Grisham (US)
Nancy Hayden (US)
Steve Jenkins(US)
Anne O'Neil (US)
Eliot Rich (US)
Frank Salvatore(US)
Bill Schindel (US)
Chris Schreiber (US)
Sharon Trauth (US)

Introduction

As a systems research analyst for Sandia National Laboratories, it was my distinct honor to lead a week-long Conversation to dig into the transformation toward a *model-based engineering* (MBE) approach with a small group of hand-picked senior systems scientist and engineers. If you don't know already, a transformation to an MBE approach is a major paradigm change for our industry, associated companies, and participating member engineers. Rarely are we offered the opportunity to thoroughly discuss these really large intractable problems. Knowing this before we started, I intentionally seeded my group with a group of professionals from diverse perspectives on the problem. The outcome of those long hours of Conversation into many diverse topics was our MBE Manifesto. I would like to propose this manifesto as a guide to motivate and possibly drive our industry toward a fully integrated digital engineering capability.

The purpose of the manifesto is to summarize and make explicit key values and principles motivating the transformation to a model-based engineering approach. We have documented in this collection of papers, the basis of our thoughts and how those concepts were incorporated into the manifesto. Each day of the Conversation is represented by articles from team members that best define the topics of discussion on that date.

The first question we often get regarding our manifesto is, "well, what do you mean by MBE?" We mean this term, model-based engineering (MBE), to be inclusive of all engineering disciplines. We fully recognize that others do not see this term in this way, but this is our meaning with the manifesto. We see the ultimate goal to be a fully digital engineering capability, and that goal must include all disciplines involved in the development of the target system. We also recognize that others do not see this as the end goal. Great, let's have a conversation about this, because clearly, this is where the industry is headed.

IFSR Conversation 2018

Background

In April 2018, a small group of senior systems engineers, scientists, and researchers assembled at the 19th IFSR Conversation in Linz, Austria, organized by the International Federation for Systems Research (IFSR), to use systems analysis methods to model a Systems Engineering approach that would optimize modern model-based engineering methods and tools. We each came from different parts of the industry and held very different perspectives on the Systems Engineering industry. The one thread that held us all together is the ideal that our industry needs to progress significantly toward a model-based approach.

We came together initially to talk about data-driven systems engineering. However, the nature of an IFSR Conversation is to allow the conversation to flow where needed. And ours flowed and ebbed in and around how we collectively felt we needed to effect a transformation toward a model-based approach.

Each of the team members were hand chosen for the extent of their different experiences in and perspectives on Systems Engineering (SE), and model-based engineering in particular.

Below is a brief description of those perspectives:

Ed Carroll: Principal R&D Systems Research Analyst at Sandia National Laboratories, and former CTO for Egghead.com. His research is focused on understanding the optimal application of advanced engineering approaches.

Dana Grisham: Principal Solutions Architect at Sandia National Laboratories. Her focus is on data architecture, software infrastructure, and governance enabling transformation to data-driven systems engineering.

Nancy Hayden, PhD: Principal R&D Systems Analyst at Sandia National Laboratories, and Research Fellow, Center for International and Security Studies at Maryland. Research focus is intersection of complexity, system dynamics, technology innovation, policy, and strategic stability.

Steve Jenkins: Principal Engineer at Jet Propulsion Laboratory and California Institute of Technology. Steve has been instrumental in developing and evangelizing an ontology-based MBSE transformation and innovation at the lab.

Anne O'Neil: Systems Catalyst and Strategist with Anne O'Neil Consultants, LLC. Anne advices organizations world-wide seeking to adopt systems practices and leverage systems engineering capability to achieve and improve business outcomes.

Eliot Rich, PhD.: Associate Professor of IS and Business Analytics, School of Business, University at Albany, SUNY. He leads the University of Albany System Dynamics Group and is an ACM Senior Member.

Frank Salvatore: Technical Fellow at Engility Corporation. Expert System Engineering Professional (ESEP) and OMG Certified Modeling Professional (OCSMP). Frank supports DOD organizations in digital engineering transformation initiatives and supports programs.

Bill Schindel: President of ICTT System Sciences, is an INCOSE Fellow, co-chair of the INCOSE MBSE Patterns Working Group, and leads application of the S*Metamodel and S*Patterns across multiple domains.

Chris Schreiber: a Systems Engineering Senior Manager for Lockheed Martin Space Systems Company with responsibility for the Systems Engineering Modernization department focused on supporting Space Systems programs with Model-Based Systems Engineering.

Sharon Trauth: Principal R&D Systems Engineer at Sandia National Laboratories, leading MBSE application to weapons, and innovating a new method to model the relationships between environmental constraints, components and their allocated functions.

Conversation Agenda Flow

In the months prior to the Conversation, the team collaborated extensively on the agenda. Our concern was to ensure that we had a week-long agenda that would produce worthwhile, engaging, and conclusive conversations. As might be expected, the resultant starting agenda was far too ambitious for time available. However, we had agreed before coming together that the agenda would be ours to manipulate and adjust as the week progressed. And indeed, the agenda did ebb and flow. Interestingly enough though, we dug deep into areas that needed to be drilled into and flew over others where we all agreed.

The flow of our conversation is depicted in this System Dynamics model in Figure 1, below:

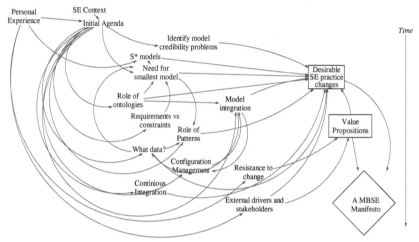

Figure 1: System dynamics model of our Conversations

The final agenda that converged at the conversation flowed through the S*Space paradigm, starting with the system model of the target system - the thing being developed (S1), working upward toward the model of life cycle domain system – the system that manages the target system model (S2), and then on to the model of system of innovation – the system that evolves the life cycle domain system (S3). Figure 2, below, illustrates this model.

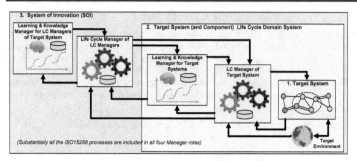

Figure 2: System of Innovation Reference Pattern (© 2016, Schindel and Dove)

The Conversations seemed to naturally flow in this direction, in that after diving deep into each topic, it seemed natural to take a step upward to resolve how that topic fit into the larger puzzle. We will discuss the S*Space paradigm more in the section on Model Credibility.

The remainder of this document is presented as a series of short articles authored by the team member who led the Conversation at that point in the agenda, giving their perspective on a particular topic which they helped introduce to the group at large, similar to an anthology.

Monday, April 9, 2018:
Model Credibility
By William Schindel, President, ICTT System Sciences

The "model situational setting" assumed here is described by another model, shown in Figure 4, illustrating a *Modeled Thing*, the *Model* that *describes* it to a *Model Interpreter* (whether human or machine), and a *Context of Use* of that model—the purpose for which the model is employed.

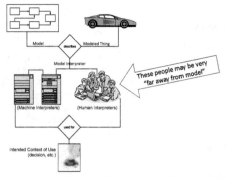

Figure 3: Model Use Situational Setting (© 2005, adapted from Schindel)

In the historical science and engineering communities, the *credibility of a model for a given use* is about more than whether that model has been "sold" to stakeholders by a compelling marketing pitch. Stated another way, the "compelling marketing pitch" takes the form of evidence meeting mathematical criteria, the nature of which is a discipline in itself—the practice of Model Verification, Validation, and Uncertainty Quantification (Model VVUQ).

Scientific and engineering models have enabled humans to predict, explain and understand, synthesize, and communicate to others an expanding fraction of the behavior of the world around us. The scientific revolution of the last three centuries, and the engineering exploitation of the knowledge it has discovered and organized, have dramatically lifted the quality, length, and possibilities of human life.

The understanding of the placement of systems engineering in the overall body of engineering practices, and of systems science in the overall body of physical sciences, is evolving in the early part of the twenty-first century. Carefully interpreted, the history of physical sciences and engineering disciplines tell us a great deal about emerging understanding of "systems", and the systems perspective in turn deepens our understanding of traditional science and engineering. Models and their credibility, or conversely model uncertainty, are at the heart of this perspective. Model VVUQ is a proxy for group scientific learning. This includes both human-synthesized "physics-based models" as well as machine learning agent based "data-driven models".

Systems engineering as a formal body of knowledge and practice has emerged over the last half-century and is younger by far than the traditional engineering disciplines (ME, EE, ChE, CE, etc.). Likewise, the systems engineering community's enthusiasm for "system models", along with its related methods, languages, and tooling has emerged and accelerated over the most recent two decades. The connections of these subjects to the related scientific and engineering theory and practices are not yet always recognized. Among these are powerful capabilities that have become relatively well-established based on their success over the much longer history of physical sciences and engineering disciplines.

The American Society of Mechanical Engineers (ASME www.asme.org) has led an expanding two-decade effort for public standardization of well-documented theory and practice for VVUQ of models across multiple technologies and application domains (Oberkampf and Roy 2010). Joined by the International Council on Systems Engineering (INCOSE www.incose.org) and others, this and related work is expanding awareness of both model VVUQ and deeper connections of models of all types (Schindel 2018a, 2018b).

At the heart of physical science is the discovery and VVUQ of phenomenon-based models, with the expectation that these learnings are accumulated and not re-learned "from scratch" repeatedly—at risk when infrastructure and practice do not encourage the effective accumulation and utilization of what is already "learned" in the form of general models. At the present time, the enthusiasm of the systems and computational modeling communities for creation of models sometimes does not fully address the question of how to take advantage of what has already been learned.

With continuing growth in application of models to high complexity, high criticality situations of use, and continuing growth in formality of model VVUQ is consequently required, the combined cost, schedule, and risk event occurrence impacts increase pressure to make more effective use of already learned, already "VVUQ'd" models—these "trusted patterns" are discussed further in later sections below. At an enterprise or industry domain level, model refinement and model VVUQ become a form of organizational learning, and a place to explicitly manage inherent uncertainty-related risks (more than just thinking of models as "truth", as "validated" or "wrong").

Figure 4, illustrates on overview of the System of Innovation Pattern, a reference adaptive/learning systems framework for analyzing, comparing, understanding, planning and improving any type of environment for accumulation and application of trusted learning. It applies to human and other biological learning, model-based engineering, advanced machine learning, and other environments:

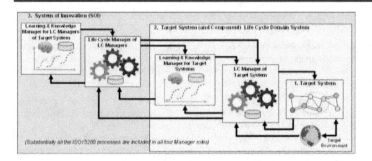

Figure 4: System of Innovation Reference Pattern (© 2016, Schindel and Dove)

In Figure 4:

- **System 1:** The "target system" is any system to be understood scientifically, engineered, or otherwise managed across its life cycle
- **System 2:** Includes the entire environment of System 1 across its life cycle, including in particular its Life Cycle Management Systems (for its planning, engineering, instantiation, operation, improvement, support, and disposal), divided into:
  - Learning & Knowledge Manage for Target System: Creates (mental or formal engineering) models of System 1 and its operating environment
  - LC Manager of Target System: Manages System 1, based on what is already known (previously learned) about System 1 and its operating environment
- **System 3:** Manages the life cycle of System 2, including learning about it and its operating environment; also, actively manages System 2 deployment and improvement based on what has been learned about System 2.

Systems engineers often refer to the ISO15288 standards for system life cycle management processes, or to the INCOSE Systems Engineering Handbook. Both of these references describe System 2 first and foremost--but the pattern of Figure 5 divides those processes into learning aspects versus execution based on what is already known. The work of INCOSE, ASME, and IFSR is largely in the roles of System 3.

"Agile methods" for engineering were developed because of inherent uncertainties, in the interest of improving the learning process to integrate it more deeply with the other aspects of engineering and life cycle management. Initially developed for use in the absence of formal models of System 1, the addition of such models makes possible the further advancement of "agile" methods to make use of the Theory of Optimal Estimation and Control—but applied to the uncertainties navigated by System 2, not System 1. Use of model-based representation of System 1 and its operating environment transforms agile methods' heuristic "next increment" selection strategy into optimal estimation and control as a basis for managing uncertainty and risk in Hilbert space.

Learning is not "flat". When it is expressed in sufficiently complete explicit models (see S*Models later below), it creates abstraction hierarchies of model-based patterns (see S*Patterns Figure G). This includes not just System 1 Patterns for engineered systems, but also System 2 Patterns for engineering, production, other life cycle management processes, including Model VVUQ itself. This provides the foundation for the Model VVUQ Pattern currently being applied in the ASME Model VV standards work.

In regulated markets (flight, medicine, automotive, food, utilities, financial), risk management through models offers future promise, depending upon community agreement to the trust in evidentiary value of those models. Model based patterns, with both general shared upper levels and company-specific lower level, offer a medium for facilitated collaboration across regulated domains, streamlining innovation.

"System level" models are frequently assumed to be different in nature than "computational models", but it is asserted here that this is primarily an accident of history. Instead, it is asserted that all of these models are inherently computational (question-answering by retrieval, query, and application) and that all of them require model VVUQ for intended uses. As argument supporting this assertion, consider the use of the Phenomena Identification and Ranking Table (PIRT) (Oberkampf and Roy 2010) for determining confidence in identification of "most important phenomena" to describe in computational models. This accepted practice applies likewise (or should), in any "systems level" model.

References

1. Schindel, W., "INCOSE Collaboration In an ASME-Led Standards Activity: Standardizing V&V of Models", in *Proc. of INCOSE MBSE Workshop*, IW2018, Jacksonville, FL, Jan, 2018.

2. Schindel, W., and Dove, R., "Introduction to the Agile Systems Engineering Life Cycle MBSE Pattern", in *Proc. of INCOSE 2016 International Symposium*, Edinburgh, UK, July, 2016.

3. Schindel, W., "Innovation, Risk, Agility, and Learning, Viewed as Optimal Control & Estimation", in *Proc. of INCOSE 2017 International Symposium*, Adelaide, UK, July, 2017.

4. Schindel, W., "MBSE Maturity Assessment: Related INCOSE & ASME Efforts, and ISO 15288", in *Proc. of MBSE Symposium*, No Magic, Inc., Allen, TX, May, 2017.

5. "ASME V&V 10-2006: Guide for Verification and Validation in Computational Solid Mechanics", ASME, 2006.

6. "ASME V&V 20-2009: Standard for Verification and Validation in Computational Fluid Dynamics and Heat Transfer", ASME, 2009.

SE knowledge Representation (Ontology)

By Steve Jenkins, Principal Engineer, Jet Propulsion Laboratory, California Institute of Technology

Introduction

Systems engineering, almost by definition, is concerned with large, complex undertakings that require multiple collaborating entities to accomplish. Consequently, systems engineering necessarily involves collection, management, and analysis of a large body of interrelated facts. Beyond whatever specific engineering discipline knowledge and expertise is required for the undertaking itself, this information management challenge requires expertise in fields more closely related to computer science, particularly knowledge representation.

Knowledge Representation is a subfield of artificial intelligence that is concerned with methods for providing high-level descriptions of the world that can be effectively used to build intelligent software applications. In this context, "intelligent" refers to the ability of a system to find implicit consequences of its explicitly-represented knowledge[1].

Knowledge Representation and MBSE

The emergence of the term *model-based systems engineering* (MBSE) has had the unfortunate effect of creating the impression that models in systems engineering are a recent development. In fact, all engineering, and indeed all applied science, is and has always been based on models of the real world. *F = ma* is a model; a breadboard circuit is a model; a digital simulation is a model. The real innovation of

MBSE is the transfer of these models from representations intended purely for human interpretation to representations using formalisms of computer and information science and intended for human *and* machine interpretation.

Unfortunately, uptake and infusion of these ideas has been slow, to the detriment of the discipline, by the fact that systems engineers have not typically studied computer science beyond elementary programming, if at all. Thus, there is a lack of awareness of powerful theory and practical technology that directly applicable to the types of problems encountered in systems engineering.

A Simple Example

Consider the problem of representing the compositional structure of a system. This representation is sometimes called a Product Breakdown Structure, or Bill of Materials (BOM). One can, of course, construct such a representation in the form of an indented list of assemblies, subassemblies, parts, etc. using office automation tools. This approach, however, suffers from a number of weaknesses:

1. A BOM is just one of many views in which these items might appear. Another important view might be a schedule that indicates when each item is available for assembly. It is cumbersome and error-prone to maintain consistency across these two views—even though they are about the same items—by referring only to item names.
2. There are rules of well-formedness for a BOM that are not enforced. For example, an item in a BOM must appear only once and can be part of at most one immediate parent item. These rules are easily violated in an indented list by simply listing an item under multiple parents.
3. There are analytical relationships implied by the tree structure that do not follow immediately from a list representation. For example, the mass of a mechanical aggregate is the sum of the masses of its immediate children, and so on for those children. Making an indented list does not itself impose the implied relationships.

Formally, a BOM can be represented as a graph data structure known as a *directed rooted tree*. Directed rooted trees manifest several invariant properties, including the second item above. In the parlance of graph theory, the vertices of the tree are the assemblies and the edges are the parent-child relationships.

Modern knowledge representation languages (e.g., OWL 2[2]) are also formally based in graph theory, so it is straightforward to define a single OWL class to correspond to BOM vertices and a single object property to correspond to edges.

For the purposes of illustration, we call the class *Component* and the object property *contains*. The names are chosen to be suggestive but otherwise have no significance. In OWL, every *named individual* is identified by an *Uniform Resource Identifier* (URI), a globally-unique name. We would probably also define properties for human-friendly local names (e.g., *rear axle assembly*) but these are peripheral to our main interest at the moment.

The essential semantics of a BOM follow from the attributes of the *contains* relationship, a mapping from *Component* to *Component*:

- inverse functional: no *Component* can be contained by more than one *Component*
- asymmetric: no *Component* can both contain and be contained by the same *Component*
- irreflexive: no *Component* can contain itself

These class and property definitions are simple in OWL:

```
Declaration(Class(:Component))

Declaration(ObjectProperty(:contains))
```

InverseFunctionalObjectProperty(:contains)

AsymmetricObjectProperty(:contains)

IrreflexiveObjectProperty(:contains)

ObjectPropertyDomain(:contains :Component)

ObjectPropertyRange(:contains :Component)

Note that the class and property definitions are completely general and apply equally well to compositions of cars, space vehicles, software, anything. That is, they could be part of a general ontology for systems engineering.

As a simple example, consider this trivial BOM:

1. rear axle assembly
   a. left rear wheel assembly
      i. left rear wheel
      ii. left rear tire
   b. left axle assembly
   c. right rear wheel assembly
      i. right rear wheel
      ii. right rear tire
   d. right axle assembly
   e. differential assembly
      i. pinion
      ii. ring gear
      iii. housing

With these earlier definitions in place it is straightforward to declare specific Components:

ClassAssertion(:Component :rearAxleAssembly)

ClassAssertion(:Component :differentialAssembly)

ClassAssertion(:Component :leftRearWheelAssembly)

ClassAssertion(:Component :rightRearWheelAssembly)

etc.

And similarly straightforward to assert specific containment relationships:

ObjectPropertyAssertion(:contains :rearAxleAssembly :differentialAssembly)

ObjectPropertyAssertion(:contains :rearAxleAssembly :leftRearWheelAssembly)

ObjectPropertyAssertion(:contains :rearAxleAssembly :rightRearWheelAssembly)

etc.

An important aspect to note is that specific applications would probably require more fine-grained distinctions than *Component* alone. In our mechanical example above, we would likely create a taxonomy of *Component* types to make distinctions at type level:

SubClassOf(:MechanicalAssembly, :Component)

SubClassOf(:AxleAssembly, :MechanicalAssembly)

SubClassOf(:RearAxleAssembly, :AxleAssembly)

etc.,

meaning every *RearAxleAssembly* is an *AxleAssembly*, every *AxleAssembly* is a *MechanicalAssembly*, and every *MechanicalAssembly* is a *Component*.

We would then assert, for example:

ClassAssertion(:RearAxleAssembly :rearAxleAssembly)

meaning the individual named *rearAxleAssembly* is a member of the class *RearAxleAssembly* (note subtle spelling difference). Every *RearAxleAssembly* is (transitively) a *Component*, so our *rearAxleAssembly* can appear in a well-formed BOM via the *contains* relationship.

This approach does not suffer from the weaknesses enumerated above:

1. Each Component is uniquely identified by its globally-unique URI. (Our examples have abbreviated the URIs for readability.) Cross-referencing is straightforward using URIs.
2. Well-formedness is enforced by the attributes of *contains*: its domain and range and the inverse functional, asymmetric, and irreflexive attributes.
3. It is simple to write a single reusable software method that, for any BOM specified using this vocabulary, constructs the applicable analytic relationships between parent and child masses. Such a rule can be written once, tested thoroughly, and applied many times.

These specific examples illustrate the use of that ontology for a particular application. The important feature to note is that the syntax and conventions for expressing a BOM in this form are specified entirely by international standards. A variety of software tools implementing aspects of these standards are available, including open source reasoners that can verify that a particular BOM satisfies all rules of well-formedness. That is, any file purporting to be a BOM can be easily and unambiguously validated using off-the-shelf tools. Agreement on these conventions suffices to establish a universal format for data exchange that preserves the semantics necessary for proper interpretation.

Systems engineering is inherently a collaborative endeavor. Consequently, standards for information interchange that simultaneously simplify communication and preserve strong semantics would be a step forward for the discipline.

A Bill of Materials is an example of a modeling pattern—a canonical structure that has widespread application and can be formally specified. There are numerous other such patterns in systems engineering: work breakdown structure, system interconnection, requirements specification, requirements flow-down, etc.

It is a straightforward (if nontrivial) exercise to repeat for these other patterns what we just did for containment:

*   Determine, by analyzing use cases, the scope of applicable knowledge and reasoning.
*   Determine the "shape" of the relevant knowledge graph and its well-formedness properties (e.g, directed, acyclic, bipartite), etc.
*   Create (or reuse existing) classes and properties that formalize the shape.

Patterns can be developed in any order, but for pedagogical purposes it is better to begin with simpler patterns (such as our containment example) and branch from there into patterns that elaborate new viewpoints. For example, a system interconnection pattern would reuse the notion of *Component* but introduce new vocabulary to represent interfaces, junctions, etc.

References

1. Nardi, D., and Brachman, R. (2007). An introduction to description logics. In F. Baader, D. Calvanese, D. McGuinness, D. Nardi, and P. Patel-Schneider (Eds.), *The description logic handbook: theory, implementation, and applications*, second edition (pp. 1-2). Cambridge: Cambridge University Press.
2. World Wide Web Consortium (2012). OWL 2 Web Ontology Language Document Overview (Second Edition).
3. Internet Engineering Task Force (1998). Uniform Resource Identifiers (URI): Generic Syntax. RFC 2396

Formalizing the Practice of Systems Engineering (representing constraints)

By Steve Jenkins, Principal Engineer, Jet Propulsion Laboratory, California Institute of Technology

A Systems Engineering Problem

Suppose some agency wishes to acquire a dataset D about a planetary body, e.g.,

- $planetary\_body(D)$ = Europa
- $spatial\_resolution(D) < r_1$
- $spectral\_resolution(D) < r_2$
- $cost(D) < C$
- $availability(D) < $ 2030-01-01

Suppose we are given the job of producing such a dataset. If we already have such a dataset, or can obtain one, we're done; no Systems Engineering is required.

If we don't already have one, we can consider the specifications of the dataset to be a set of requirements, i.e., constraints to be satisfied. Let's call this set R_1. Unless we know how to satisfy R_1 directly, we have to transform our problem into a set of problems that we know how to solve and imply the solution of the original problem. That is, we need to find another set of constraints C_2 that can, at least in principle, be satisfied (that's what "we know how to solve" means) and that suffice for R_1 (that's what "imply the solution of the original problem" means).

This is where engineering comes in.

The Nature of Engineering

Engineering is about solving practical problems, e.g.,

- There's water here and there shouldn't be.
- There isn't water here and there should be.
- It's dark and cold here.
- I have a message for people far away.

Engineering is distinguished from many other fields of endeavor by its reliance on science and mathematics, and consequently, its rigor. Our scientific knowledge plus our experience help us understand how to decompose a problem we can't solve into others we can.

Elaborating Constraints

We don't know how to satisfy R_1 directly, but

- We know how to build a rocket that can accelerate a payload.
- We know how to design a trajectory that will get close to Europa.
- We know how to steer a rocket to follow a trajectory.
- We know how to build instruments that measure things about planets.
- We know how to point instruments at interesting targets.
- We know how to communicate data over solar system distances.
- etc.

So, let's mount a science mission to Europa by decomposing the problem along these lines:

Figure 5: Europa Decomposition Model

This decomposition tree is the *Work Breakdown Structure* of the mission. Literally, it is the way we (engineers) have decided to decompose the work into soluble units. It's useful for accounting, but it doesn't belong to accountants. It's the most important and most fundamental Systems Engineering work product.

The decomposition itself is another constraint set. The elements in the decomposition (e.g., launch vehicle, spacecraft, instruments, etc.) and their interactions are also described by constraints:

- Assignments to and bounds on parameters and state variables, e.g.,
    - Choice of Ka-band for data communications
    - Allocation of electric power for telecom
- Laws of physics and chemistry, e.g.,
    - Inverse square law
    - Noise power and spectrum
- Engineering analysis results, e.g.,
    - Phase-locked loop receiver performance
    - Error-correcting code performance

C_2 contains two types of constraints:

- Those that are satisfied (or at least we take to be satisfied)
    - Things that we make satisfied by *fiat*, i.e., engineering design choices. Analysis tells us how to make good (sometimes optimal) choices, but in the end they are choices.

o Invariants of the real world, i.e., facts. Our models of the real world are often choices as well, e.g., linearization of more complex relationships (e.g., Ohm's Law). Having chosen a model, its implications are taken as satisfied for the purpose of analysis.
- Things that, if satisfied, would make C_2 sufficient for R_1, that is, whatever we have to add to show by analysis that C_2 implies R_1.

Returning to our example, we have gone from a set of constraints on a data set (R_1) to another set of constraints about propulsion, navigation, telecom, etc. (C_2). Among the constraints in C_2 are:

- Choices we have made (e.g., Ka-band telemetry, coding & modulation, etc.)
- Facts (e.g., inverse-square law, Shannon's Theorem, etc.)

If we're smart enough, we'll be able to deduce a further set of constraints (on, for example, telecom performance) that, when combined with our decisions and facts, suffice for R_1. These additional constraints are *requirements*. They aren't necessarily satisfied; we want to make them satisfied; call them R_2.

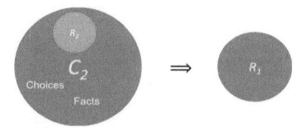

Figure 6: Constraints Deduced To Requirements

That's the kind of problem we started with. We started with R_1, a set of constraints to be satisfied. We developed C_2, containing Choices, Facts, and Requirements (R_2). We showed by analysis that C_2 implies R_1 and R_2 implies C_2. Therefore, if R_2 is satisfied, then C_2 is satisfied and R_1 is satisfied.

We can address the requirements R_2 exactly the way we addressed R_1. The process repeats recursively, terminating when we reach a requirement set R_n that we can satisfy with choices and facts alone in C_{n+1}, e.g., selecting an off-the-shelf device whose operating characteristics suffice for R_n. Then

$$C_{n+1} \Longrightarrow R_n \Longrightarrow C_n \Longrightarrow \ldots \Longrightarrow R_2 \Longrightarrow C_2 \Longrightarrow R_1$$

Problem solved.

A final observation about requirements and constraints: a requirement *is* a constraint. It isn't necessarily satisfied (e.g., a true fact). Moreover, we can't satisfy it by fiat (a choice). If we could, we would simply do so. Our remaining option at this point is to engage another party (a supplier) who will offer to satisfy it, generally in return for some consideration. More succinctly, requirements are those constraints we have delegated to a supplier to satisfy on our behalf.

Tuesday, April 10, 2018:
Validation and Verification of Model for Complex Systems

By Eliot Rich, University at Albany, Dept. of Information Systems and Business Analytics, Albany, NY

When is a model a good model? As models serve as abstractions of reality, good models capture the important factors of the underlying system while omitting characteristics that are less important to the user. During our discussions of model-based engineering two interesting observations emerged. First, both model uses and model users change during their lifetime. Second, modeling is a social process as well as an engineering one. Both have effects on the adoption of model-based engineering and the successful completion of complex projects.

The defining characteristics of complex systems is their dynamism. Change occurs in unforeseen ways, whether it be through emergent behaviors, feedback and accumulation, or changes in the environment in which they are embedded. Dynamic models capture and predict change over time and are requisite for complex systems. A static model, one that has no mechanisms for recognizing endogenous change, cannot fully capture when change occurs and how it affects the predicted behavior being modeled. This does not mean a static model, such as some key indicator of performance, is unsuitable. Rather, the modeler should recognize that part of what is being abstracted is change over time, such as degradation or interactions with other components. It may or may not be important to the short-term task but as the complexity of the problem grows, dynamics become more and more relevant.

Model users also change over time as systems mature and move into new modes. The engineering diagrams developed during design live well beyond their initial purpose as components are combined to produce new and potentially unanticipated products, and as products move through their life cycles. Maintenance, replacement, re-sourcing, and retooling changes the types of information needed to sustain the product.

I assert that models of complex systems must consider the same dynamism that underlies the systems themselves. In the systems engineering world the concept of VVUQ (Verification, Validation, and Uncertainty Quantification) [1] relies on the ability to ascertain that the model and its representation adequately capture the behavior of the system of interest. But how does the modeler bound their VVUQ efforts when the future environment is not known, or more pragmatically, when project delivery pressures may limit the resources available to cover the universe of possible uses?

The response to this question is to clearly define what is known about the model and its suitability at the time of its development. VVUQ is a form of trust building exercise. We need to be clear about the model's boundaries. Clear use cases, explicit and reproducible test conditions, and a consistent taxonomy are all necessary to document what the model captures, and perhaps more importantly, what it does not capture. Subsequent users of models need to retain a degree of skepticism of the work of their predecessors and be given the means to review and confirm the suitability of the models for new purposes.

There is also an opportunity to extend the purpose of the VVUQ to consider potential futures for the systems they are capturing. Stakeholders and modelers can combine their efforts to consider where the boundaries of the system may extend beyond the immediate and identify potential futures for their work, and how their efforts may be reused. This extension builds upon the S* concept [2] to integrate learning and reuse of models and concepts over time.

Modelers are therefore working towards the resolution of their own objectives, and at the same time are unknowingly serving the objectives of others. Here is where the social nature of validation arises, as requirements and use cases will span disciplinary definitions of suitability to purpose. This adds another argument to the need for transparency about what testing and validation accomplish. Treating engineering of complex systems as a set of parallel but independent domains will need to yield to pressures for communication, boundary-spanning activities, and techniques to establish and preserve shared meaning. Systems Engineers cannot master all fields of engineering. Rather, they will generate benefit from learning various systems thinking approaches that bring multiple stakeholders with relevant but different perspectives into the validation process. As yet another dynamic process, the introduction of systems thinking and systems modeling techniques will not happen with a mandate or a specification alone. The introduction will rely on first establishing the need, successful interventions and implementations, and subsequent diffusion over time, integrating lessons from each iteration as well as any missteps.

Will the creator of a model spend time and effort to test theory work beyond the edges of what their needs demand? That's a big ask, particularly when complexity comes into play. Who knows what the model and its underlying system will be used for in the future? This may be a key contribution of the Systems Engineering profession, where integration and prediction play a role that might not be as visible within singular disciplines. It may also be an area where intelligent automation can expand the range and the efficiency of exploration of uncertain model uses based on historical usage.

References

[1]   W. D. Schindel, "Standardizing V&V of Models," presented at the 2018 Annual INCOSE International Workshop, Jacksonville, FL, 2018.

[2]   W. D. Schindel, S. A. Lewis, J. J. Sherey, and S. K. Sanyal, "Accelerating MBSE Impacts Across the Enterprise: Model-Based S*Patterns," *INCOSE International Symposium*, vol. 25, pp. 1159-1176, 2015.

What Is the Smallest Model of a System?

(adapted from (Schindel 2011))

By William Schindel, President, ICTT System Sciences

The size of a model is of theoretical interest because the size of a system's "minimal representation" is one definition of its complexity. A more practical engineering interest is that the size and redundancy of engineering specifications challenge the effectiveness of systems engineering processes. Humankind needs to find the simplest—but not too simple--approaches to systems engineering. Practitioner MBSE models are often too large and too small at once--missing key information while redundant in other aspects.

An S*Model is any model of any type that conforms to the S*Metamodel. The S*Metamodel is a tool-neutral, modeling language-neutral underlying metamodel that was developed over several decades of practice, starting with the question "What is the smallest model necessary for the traditional purposes of science and engineering?" It is an underlying reference frame that has been mapped to and applied using numerous commercial modeling tools and modeling languages (Schindel 2011):

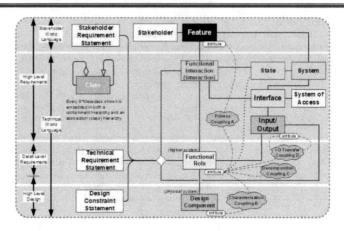

Figure 7: S*Metamodel Summary (© 2018, 2011, Schindel)

There is an unfortunate perception that "system models" are of a different nature than "discipline-specific models", arising from the peculiar history of SE compared to the other disciplines. Other engineers believe their discipline is based on "fundamental" physical laws (e.g., mechanics), and that SE is not phenomena-based. The more useful perspective is a converse: The System Phenomenon and Hamilton's Principle are the basis of all the other disciplines' "laws". In particular, this says not to omit Interactions. (Schindel 2018)

Modeled Patterns

An S*Pattern is an S*Model that is re-usable and configurable to different situations, applications, customer segment, product line element, or other specific. Pattern-Based Systems Engineering (PBSE) is a form of Model-Based Systems Engineering (MBSE) that is based upon such reusable S*Patterns (see Figure 6).

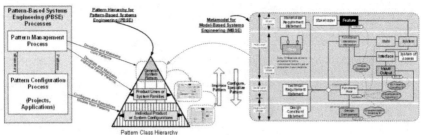

Figure 8: PBSE, Using Model-Based S*Pattern (© 2011, Schindel)

Pattern-Based Systems Engineering is MBSE with an emphasis on _trusted_ shared enterprise and domain community models which are configurable to particular situations or applications. Instead of the traditional MBSE emphasis on "learn _to_ model", the emphasis of PBSE is "learn _the_ model". Refer to Figure 7:

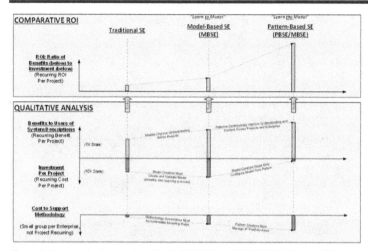

Figure 9: Comparative Economics of Basic SE, MBSE, and PBSE (© 2011, Schindel)

Model-based System Patterns, organized by Gestalt Rules, divide system descriptions into fixed and variable parts, further compressing models, and enabling PBSE. The Minimum Description Length Principle helps compress models and model space representation. Refer to Figure 8.

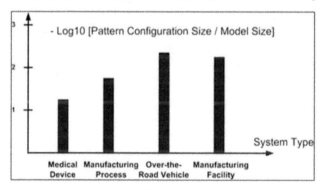

Figure 10: Degree of Model Compression by S*Patterns (© 2011, Schindel)

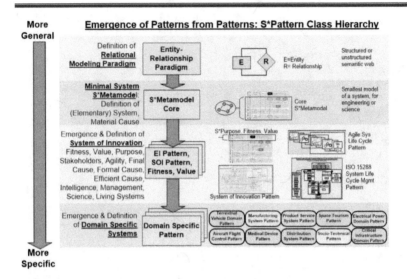

More General

Emergence of Patterns from Patterns: S*Pattern Class Hierarchy

More Specific

Figure 11: S*Pattern Hierarchy, General to Specific (© 2011, Schindel)

References

1. INCOSE Model-Based Transformation web site:
   https://www.incose.org/about/strategicobjectives/transformation

2. Beihoff, B., et al, "A World in Motion: INCOSE Vision 2025", INCOSE, 2014.
   vhttps://www.incose.org/docs/default-source/aboutse/se-vision-2025.pdf

3. "INCOSE MBSE Transformation Planning & Assessment Framework: Beta Test":
   http://www.omgwiki.org/MBSE/lib/exe/fetch.php?media=mbse:patterns:planning_assessment_
   requirements_for_mbse_model_applications_v1.4.2.pdf

4. Schindel, Morrison, Pellettiere, Donaldson, Peterson, Heller, Johnson, "Panel: Accelerating Innovation Effectiveness--Model-Facilitated Collaboration by Regulators, Technical Societies, Customers, and Suppliers", in *Proc. of INCOSE 2018 International Symposium*, Washington, DC, July, 2018.

5. Schindel, W., and Dove, R., "Introduction to the Agile Systems Engineering Life Cycle MBSE Pattern", in *Proc. of INCOSE 2016 International Symposium*, Edinburgh, UK, July, 2016.

6. Schindel, W., "Innovation, Risk, Agility, and Learning, Viewed as Optimal Control & Estimation", in *Proc. of INCOSE 2017 International Symposium*, Adelaide, UK, July, 2017.

7. INCOSE Patterns Working Group, "MBSE Methodology Summary: Pattern-Based Systems Engineering (PBSE), Based On S*MBSE Models", V1.5.5A, retrieve from: http://www.omgwiki.org/MBSE/doku.php?id=mbse:pbse

8. INCOSE MBSE Patterns Working Group web site, at:
   http://www.omgwiki.org/MBSE/doku.php?id=mbse:patterns:patterns

IFSR Conversation 2018

9. J. Sherey, "Capitalizing on Systems Engineering", *Proceedings of the INCOSE 2006 International Symposium*, Orlando, FL, July, 2006.

10. Schindel, W., "Got Phenomena? Science-Based Disciplines for Emerging Systems Challenges", in *Proc. of INCOSE 2017 International Symposium*, Adelaide, UK, 2017.

11. Schindel, W., "Requirements Statements Are Transfer Functions: An Insight from Model-Based Systems Engineering", in *Proc. of INCOSE 2005 International Symposium*, Rochester, NY, 2005.

12. Grunwald, P. 2007. *The Minimum Description Length Principle*. Cambridge, MA: MIT Press.

13. Schindel, W., "Hamilton's Principle and Noether's Theorem as a Basis for System Science", in *Proc. of INCOSE 2018 International Workshop, System Sciences Working Group, Jacksonville, FL, Jan, 2018*.

Using Data

By Frank Salvatore, Technical Fellow, Engility Corporation

At the foundation of a model driven Systems Engineering approach is the data. The data needs to be known for this approach to work. It needs to be defined early on, managed and controlled. A data model needs to contain that definition so that it can be communicated. The data needs to be planned for and supported as it matures throughout a programs life cycle. Today's systems engineering teams supporting development efforts are taking a model-based approach in order to be able to improve communications, and manage the increased complexity found in systems being built. This is a major trend across the globe in all industries. As part of this trend not only is the Systems Engineering discipline refining it's practices but it is also finding that in order to practice the discipline of systems engineering there is a need to communicate consistently across domains.

The IFSR session recognized the need to include the use of data in this conversation and invited the Office of the Secretary of Defense (OSD), Office Under the Secretary of Defense (OUSD) for Research and Engineering (R-E) who had some efforts in play focusing on data and its use. OSD recognized the need to focus on the data and developed a data taxonomy as a place to start (Zimmerman, 2017) . In an effort to build acceptance of the data taxonomy OSD brought it to the 2017 INCOSE International Workshop (IW) to review and critique it. They held two sessions at this IW.

One session centered on reviewing and commenting on the data taxonomy (Zimmerman, 2017). For the most part the taxonomy was reasonably accepted and only minor changes were made to it as a result.

The second session, hosted by the Decision Analysis Working Group (DAWG), focused on the use of the data in support of decision analysis activities thru the *Air Force Materiel Command, Digital Thread Workshop*. In this workshop it became clear that there needed to be more definition around data in artifacts and how those artifacts were exchanged between members of a project team.

The workshop revealed that project teams worked with data from across multiple parties to gather data that was often found inconsistent and or incomplete. The workshop revealed that there was not a clear understanding of how the data flowed amongst, between, and thru the artifacts to support decision analysis activities.

As a result a *Digital Artifacts challenge team* was formed which now has evolved into the *Digital Engineering Information Exchange Working Group (DEIXWG)*. The DEIXWG is currently working to provide definition of terms in the *Topical Encyclopedia for Digital Engineering Information Exchange (DEIXPedia), Digital Engineering Information Exchange Model (DEIXM), Digital Viewpoint Model (DVM) , DEIX Standards Framework* products that will help to improve the acquisition, flow, and delivery of data amongst people and objects that use it. Having more definition of data that can flow affords the benefits of improved automation and better integration. Having data enables automated, understanding of quality of the data. The IFSR built upon these effort in its conversation around using data.

References

1. Philomena Zimmerman, "Modeling the Digital System Model Data Taxonomy", 20th Annual NDIA Systems Engineering Conference, Springfield, VA, October 25, 2017, available online at: https://www.acq.osd.mil/se/briefs/19906-NDIA17-Zimm-DSMTax.pdf
2. Philomena Zimmerman, "DoD Digital Engineering, Digital System Model (DSM) Workshop", 2017 INCOSE International Workshop, Jan 29, 2017.
3. Digital Engineering Information Exchange Working Group (DEIXWG), available online at: http://www.omgwiki.org/MBSE/doku.php?id=mbse:deix
4. Topical Encyclopedia for Digital Engineering Information Exchange (DEIXPedia), available online at: http://www.omgwiki.org/MBSE/doku.php?id=mbse:topical_encyclopedia_for_digital_engineering_information_exchange_deixpedia
5. Digital Engineering Information Exchange Model (DEIXM), available online at: http://www.omgwiki.org/MBSE/doku.php?id=mbse:digital_engineering_information_exchange_model
6. *Digital Viewpoint Model (DVM), available online at: http://www.omgwiki.org/MBSE/doku.php?id=mbse:digital_viewpoint_model_dvm*
7. DEIX Standards Framework, available online at: http://www.omgwiki.org/MBSE/doku.php?id=mbse:deix_standards_framework

Data-driven Optimization

By Nancy Hayden, PhD, Principal R&D Systems Analyst, Sandia National Laboratories

System optimization through tradeoff analyses applied throughout the design and engineering life cycle is a key element of systems engineering required to balance cost, schedule, and technical objectives. One of the challenges in optimizing systems is to define appropriate measures and indicators for tradeoff analyses across multiple system levels; and to create a framework and processes for optimizing within and across levels that (1) use consistent (or at the very least, compatible) measures and indicators; and (2) avoid convergence to locally optimal but globally sub-optimal solutions (and vice versa). The principles and values called out in the MBE Manifesto offer ways to address these challenges.

Technical Performance Measurements (TPM) defined at the start of a program at each assist in decision-making to optimize projected system (and sub-system) performance, schedule, and resource trade-offs; to identify potential technical conflicts or problems; and to assess impacts of proposed changes on system performance. Commonly used TPMs include Key Performance Parameters (KPPs), Key System Attributes (KSAs), Measures of Effectiveness (MOEs), and Measures of Performance (MOPs). [1] Traditional wisdom is that TPM parameters that especially need to be tracked are those that are cost drivers, those that lie on the critical path, and those that present high technical risk items.

KPPs are considered the most essential for successful mission accomplishment. KPPs flow from operational requirements and represent those capabilities or characteristics so significant that failure to meet the threshold value of performance can be cause for the concept or system selected to be reevaluated, or the program to be reassessed or terminated. Trade studies may typically trade off everything *except* a KPP. [2] Examples of KPPs defined by the DOD are: Force

Protection, System Survivability, Sustainment, Net-Ready, Training, Energy, and, in some cases, Nuclear Weapon Survivability.

The DOD defines Kpps as "Performance attributes of a system considered critical or essential to the development of an effective military capability." A KPP normally has a threshold representing the minimum acceptable value achievable at low-to-moderate risk, and an objective, representing the desired operational goal but at higher risk in cost, schedule, and performance. Failure of a system to meet a validated KPP threshold value triggers a review by the validation authority and evaluation of operational risk and/or military utility of the associated system(s) if KPP threshold values are not met. The review may result in validation of an updated KPP threshold value, modification of production increments, or recommendation for program cancellation.

KSAs are essential attributes for an effective capability but not selected as KPPs. KSAs provide decision makers with an additional level of capability prioritization below the KPP. A KSA does not have to be related to a KPP and there is no implication that multiple KSA's equal a KPP.

MOEs (which may be qualitative or quantitative) measure how well a mission, operational task or task element is accomplished using a system in its expected environment. The measure of the degree-to-which a system performs - MOP – can contribute to an MOE as one of a number of possible measures of how well a system's task is accomplished. MOPs can be accumulated to assess an MOE that is not directly measurable, and several MOPs may be related to the achievement of a particular MOE.

MBE offers three advantages for data-driven system optimization using TPMs. First, Key decision-makers must be able to connect what is being measured to what they need to know and what decisions they need to make as part of a closed loop, feedback process. MBE clarifies that relationship between what is measured as a TPM and key design trade-off decisions. In so doing, *Information* is advanced over *artifacts*. Moreover, MBE facilitates transparent and holistic consideration of elements moving through automated review checkpoints against TPMs, and authorization into future phases based on a check of the current state of the product against optimal as well as pre-determined thresholds based on product maturity. This reduces ambiguity – advancing *expressiveness and rigor* over *flexibility*.

Finally, MBSE facilitates the *integration* of TPMs across target subsystems to calculate and compare trade-offs within optimal solutions of individual target subsystems with those for the integrated system level in a traceable and transparent process. This could be done in a variety of ways, including the construction of objective functions from the TPMs at various system levels to help designers and decision-makers identify where locally optimal solutions may lead to sub-optimal solutions of the whole. MBE facilitates analysis of how changes to design elements might affect the optimization of system as a whole.

TPMs used in this way for optimization within MBE contribute to better understanding of *Essential invariant* dimensions of produced information. The focus on methods for transparent, system performance assessment keeps the emphasis on the *intended use* of information; and provides basis for *common and integrated understanding* among diverse decision-makers and design engineers for iterative design adequacy and trade-offs analysis.

References:
[1] Roedler, G. and C. Jones. 2005. *Technical Measurement Guide*, version 1.0. San Diego, CA, USA: International Council on Systems Engineering (INCOSE). INCOSE-TP-2003-020-01

[2] John Hopkins Whiting School of Engineering, https://ep.jhu.edu/about-us/news-and-media/explaining-kpps-ksas-moes-and-mops

[3] Defense Acquisition University, https://www.dau.mil/glossary/pages/3043.aspx

Wednesday, April 11, 2018:

Model Configuration Management (MCM)

By Sharon Trauth, Principal R&D Systems Engineer, Sandia National Laboratories

By Dana Grisham: Principal Solutions Architect at Sandia National Laboratories

The team members found that MCM was an essential discipline that was fundamental to:

- Integration of MBSE functional models with other models (MCAD, ECAD, physics-based models, etc.)
- How to enable integration with models created by other companies
- What data, what artifacts?
- How model-based techniques/metrics support the critical elements of the 'V'
- Maturing data-driven SE artifacts into a continuous integration model (comparable to the approach used in agile software projects)
- Configuration Management – in a continuous integration process

Key aspects of Configuration Management (CM) assure that changes are properly authorized and systemically incorporated. Todays' CM systems maintain information regarding change authorizations and effectivity along with the need for baseline updates correlated to changes. One key intent of CM is to assure that documentation is both accurate and consistent with the actual physical design of the item. Realization of the latter aspect can be heavily dependent on manual approaches and is likely not sustainable as our systems grow in complexity.

As the ISFR Conversation evolved, our team discussed the extension of traditional CM principals to modeling approaches. It became apparent to the Team that model integration and ultimately the confidence level we can have in "a" model is innately dependent on how we approach MCM. Our confidence level is dependent not only on the accuracy of any individual model or artifact created throughout the system life cycle, but also on our ability to ascertain the degree to which any individual model or artifact is accurately and conceptually related to any other model or artifact, and to the system they are intended to represent.

If a collection of models and their artifacts are known to relate correctly to each other and we can confirm that this collection adequately represents the current version of system we intend it to represent, then we can be more confident in using the collection to make appropriate decisions about the system and its suitability for its intended purpose. If we also expect the system to remain viable over time, we must be able to incorporate corrections or design changes; to do so we must have confidence that we are starting with the correct set of models and artifacts so as not to inadvertently introduce more errors over time and ultimately degrade the system.

To illustrate these concepts, consider Figure 12 as a (significantly) simplified illustration of the interconnectedness of models. System A is decomposed into 2 subsystems, A and B. Each of these subsystems could have a full palate of the possible models, but only a few are represented. To create an adequate thermal or radiation model, modelers may start with a simplified mechanical model, for example eliminating detailed threaded holes for mounting screws, if they are not deemed significant to the model being created. When this occurs, an alternate simplified mechanical model is created. When making decisions based on that radiation analysis, individuals need assurance that the analysis stems from a correct representation of the system. For example, if the material used in the mechanical model was changed, but the simplified model used for the radiation analysis was not changed, the findings and predictions could be invalidated.

Unless MCM provides assurances that the various models for a system, subsystem, component, or piece part are integrated and properly related, our data repositories would capture a mere aggregation of independently generated models and our level of confidence, or trust, in the model would be limited. We would rather have an integrated collection of models that provide meaningful and useful information about a system, but getting to that level of knowledge base requires effort. The distinction between these two approaches naturally leads to a discussion of the role of V&V in improving trust in the model.

Conducting V&V activities on models themselves (or on their exported artifacts) can be a laborious manual process plagued with walkthroughs, line-by-line content reviews, text or document inspections, and the like. As the complexity of our systems and their models grows, it follows that continued reliance on merely manual methods to gain confidence in our models cannot continue to suffice. Alternate approaches to verifying and validating physics-based models have been utilized, such as comparison to other trusted results or comparison with test results, and quantification of uncertainties. Our team proposed that, for models to be more trusted, we need to invest in alternate methods to assess model credibility, including machine checks for trusted patterns, reuse of known/trusted models, and conformance to trusted model standards.

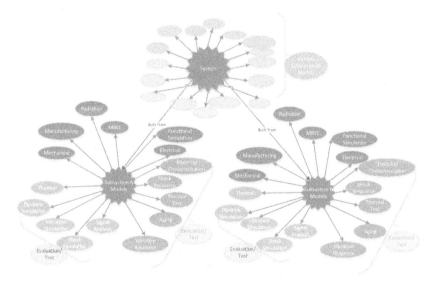

Figure 12: Model Aggregation and Integration

When different, distinct organizations (such as contractors, partners, or different groups within a single business entity) generate models that must be integrated, modeling standards and V&V methods used to establish model credibility become increasingly important. In fact, our team identified the need to establish a common semantic ontology and associated formats for the model-based data. This semantic data model is critical to being able to integrate the models beyond an aggregate collection and to being able to move from a document-based paradigm into a model-based paradigm. Such a standard ontology is also fundamental to establishing the capability to auto-generate document artifacts or other consumable visualizations on an as-needed basis from the integrated model-based content. The ontology captures and defines the entities, the entity attributes, the syntax for relating one entity to another, and the standard format for the exchange of the entities and their relationships. Figure 2 illustrates the role these ontological standards play in integrating and exchanging model-based information in a collaborative environment.

As system complexity increases, the ability of humans to manually check each model and its associated artifacts becomes significantly compromised. The existence of a semantic ontology supports the implementation of a "rules engine," as is found in currently available semantic web technologies. A rules engine enables the ontology to be inspected, measured, and acted upon with or without human interaction. The rules can be very simple, such as ensuring a given data entity has the required attributes, or they can be very complex (when paired with software algorithms), such as understanding the pattern and constraints on what constitutes "normal" and taking corrective action if something is seen as out of the bounds of the expected normal.

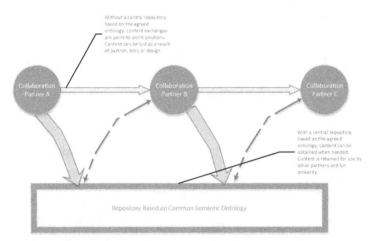

Figure 13: Semantic Ontology Enables Effective Exchange and Content Retention

The importance of these automated rules engines becomes apparent as well as we consider some of the principals and methods for agile software development. Agile methods include evolutionary requirements and product development coupled with continuous improvement; it follows that, when we utilize modeling and simulation to enhance and accelerate product development cycles, we need a reliable, continuous integration approach to MCM. Such an approach will be obviously heavily dependent on automation. Thus, a proper semantic ontology and associated rules engines, as just discussed, are key enablers to the desired shortened development cycles. As rules engines evolve to include more complex and "trusted" patterns, our reliance upon the automated MCM checks is likely to grow, as will our collection of trusted models.

Once we begin to build an integrated collection of trusted models, those models can contribute to our increased confidence in any associated analytical or behavioral predictions. However, effective means to assure that our "trusted models" remain "trusted" throughout the evolving system life cycle necessitates not only managing integrated sets of models, but also managing changes to those models such that any given integrated set remains integrated and appropriately related to our systems – two characteristics important to sustaining the desired confidence levels in our models. As a design evolves, the design architecture changes, interfaces change, models and their interconnectedness changes as well. The MCM system will need to demonstrate effective methods for keeping track of the changes and provide methods to explore the impact of proposed changes. Further, when a change that is thought to be "minor" is implemented, the MCM system needs to provide a means to confirm that associated interconnections between the models and artifacts remain viable.

As our traditional document CM approaches are extended into a model-based paradigm, along with transitioning the engineering processes themselves, our MCM methods will not only have to capture metadata about models and model elements, but also record information regarding their pedigree to establish a confidence level in the model set. Model pedigree, or provenance, information is a byproduct of the MCM approach and, if captured well, plays a role in "understandability" of the overall model as well as each of its elements. Another aspect to "understandability" that ultimately impacts model reuse is to capture the modeling process as well as key decisions and rationale by the modelers throughout their process. This information should be captured as metadata that is linked to affected model elements as well as the overall model. In essence, the full scope of what is encapsulated within a model or perhaps we call it a "model package", must include its pedigree, any automated rule checks, and other associated V&V content. The full capture of this information will assist with model integration and reuse. Whether such content is considered part of MCM or as part of model V&V, such additional measures will help assure that we develop more useful knowledge content rather than simply generating new forms of "artifacts" (aka, models) to capture for posterity.

To that end, the engineering community must transition their concepts of those forms encapsulated "knowledge" can take. For many in the current paradigm of the field, knowledge content is a document. As we transition to a more mature form of MBSE, the systems engineering community is naturally struggling to break-free of the document-based norms for providing data in context. The natural tendency is for modelers and stakeholders to take model content and produce point-in-time documents from the model to represent the system at important gates and milestones. Conversely, another approach taken by the modeling community has been to simply provide the model itself to a variety of stakeholders to let them access or export any content they desire. This approach has proven to be a not-very-consumable approach, especially for those stakeholders that are not modelers themselves. Instead, the modeling community must change from thinking about delivering a "model" to delivering information contained within a model. This paradigm shift removes the artificial constraint on our current visualization approaches: a model becomes "information" that can be queried and displayed in a multitude of ways, instead of a concept that is tightly coupled to its visual representations.

References

1. Configuration Management, https://en.wikipedia.org/wiki/Configuration_management
2. Agile Software Development, https://en.wikipedia.org/wiki/Agile_software_development

Thursday, April 12, 2018:

Paradigm Change – Artificial Intelligence and Human-Machine Interactions

By Nancy Hayden, PhD, Principal R&D Systems Analyst, Sandia National Laboratories

Technical advancements in Artificial Intelligence (AI) and their convergence in autonomous systems are revolutionizing all aspects of society, including the processes by which we work, learn, discover, and communicate. AI as used here is broadly characterized as "intelligence exhibited by machines" (JASON Report, 2017), where intelligence is "that quality that enables an entity to function appropriately and with foresight in its environment" (Stone, 2016). Autonomy can be characterized as the "capability of a system to independently compose and select among different courses of action to accomplish goals based on knowledge and understanding of the world, itself, and the situation (Defense Science Board, 2016). AI, along with massive data sets generated by the Internet of Things (IoT) and advancements in graphical processing units (GPUs) that enable computer vision for rapid imagery analysis - is a key enabler for autonomy. Autonomy, in turn, enables engineered systems to learn, adapt, and be self-governing.

Driven by exponentially increasing availability of big data and advances in hardware to support data analytics, AI applications are growing exponentially in virtually all sectors of the economy to increase productivity, effectiveness, efficiency, and capabilities beyond those of humans alone. Examples include predictive analytics for enterprise management in marketing, human resource and supply chain decisions; improving consistency and effectiveness of public service offerings and judgements through better contextual and historical analysis; and improving operational safety, productivity and efficiency through more precise, efficient, and persistent embedded diagnostic and control systems in manufacturing, health care and transportation systems. These applications are also spurring research and development in the field of Human-Machine Interactions (HMI) to better understand cognitive and behavioral impacts of AI, most efficient balances between humans and machines using AI, and most effective means for communicating and building trust between machines and humans.

Advancements in AI can enable the systems engineering community to offer new classes of solutions that could not have been realized before now. Potential advantages include increased computational efficiencies (e.g., optimized mesh generation); discovery of novel designs (e.g., generative engineering), anticipation of unanticipated and changing situations for enhanced system optimization procedures, and validation and verification processes that utilize machine learning to explore parameter spaces too complex for human understanding alone, and correctly generalizing systems engineering solutions to new settings/contexts. There are three key challenges to the adoption of AI by the systems engineering community that MBE helps to address: data requirements; the infrastructure and architecture to efficiently process data between different engineering subsystem models; and effective human-machine interactions to facilitate optimal performance and address issues of trust and transparency.

Most AI technologies in use today – such as those used for machine learning (ML) and computer vision - require massive amounts of digital data (structured and unstructured). Recent advancements in hardware that enable rapid, on-board processing of huge data sets have spurred the development of special architectures for ML algorithms, such as those required for Deep Neural Networks (DNN). These architectures are composed of multiple levels of non-linear operations, such as in neural networks with many hidden layers, each requiring significant amounts of training data that significantly impact the precision, accuracy, and extensibility of the algorithms.

Using a framework such as that shown in the figure below, the data-centric, structured environment of MBE facilitates the adoption of state-of-the art AI and Autonomy by the systems engineering community while providing a structured environment for managing AI usage and data (including training data) across system components.

AI and autonomy technologies may be embedded in the design of components for Target System 1 - as in the case of autonomous vehicles - and used in design analysis – as in the case of generative design - to predict and optimize TPMs for these technologies under a variety of conditions. AI can be used in System 2 as collaborator for learning and optimization analysis and life cycle management under a variety of configurations and uses of System 1 and its components. Finally, AI can be used in System 3 as a co-manager to innovate, integrate across multiple life-cycle domains. These applications need to be agile and robust, while simultaneously addressing new challenges in uncertainty quantification (UQ), verification and validation (V&V), and trust and assurance that provide transparency and explain-ability. Data for learning through AI within S1, S2, and S3 and the knowledge generated can be communicated to and applied between them as shown in the upper right portion of the figure.

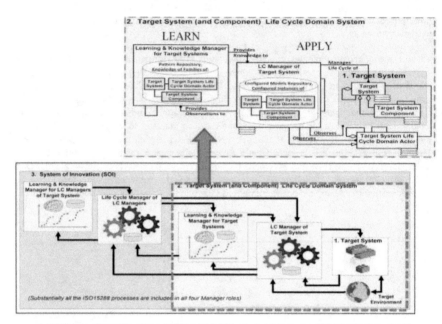

Article: Paradigm Change – Artificial Intelligence and Human-Machine Interactions

Figure 14: Adoption of State-of-the-Art AI and Autonomy by the SE Community

Studies show that AI and autonomy are most successful when effectively teamed with humans, rather than used to completely replace them (Endsley, 2016). Human-machine interactions (HMI) are key to all of these uses, involving elements of trust, transparency, and effective communication about when and how AI is being used, and for what purpose. The trust relationship for effective HMI in S1 requires that the AI-enabled system can demonstrate that it will perform transparently, reliably and predictably under anticipated conditions, and will gracefully degrade or re-allocate when unable to perform tasks. The Trust relationship required of HMI in S2 requires that AI can demonstrably provide unbiased and complete insights that accurately assist the engineering team anticipate requirements for life cycle management and dynamics under variety of complex conditions. The Trust relationship require of HMI for S3 is that AI will enhance understanding and discovery to better communicate, collaborate and share critical information about engineering processes in a timely manner.

Employing AI in these ways requires a significant paradigm shift and effective HMI that provides transparency into the reasoning for how AI is used within S1, S2, and S3; how the appropriate balance between humans and machines is being assessed; and flexibility to shift that balance. Our MBE Manifesto supports this shift. By emphasizing *information* over artifacts; we raise the value AI to the engineering process for its contributions to knowledge generation within S1, S2, and S3. By emphasizing *integration* over independence, we raise the value of AI to the engineering process for its contributions to managing complexity. By emphasizing *model usage* over model creation, we highlight the role that MBE can play in designing effective HMI for building transparency and trust in AI that is incorporated into the system engineering process.

References

Perspectives on Research in Artificial Intelligence and Artificial General Intelligence Relevant to DoD, JASON, The MITRE Corporation, p. 1, January 2017.

Stone, P., et al. Artificial Intelligence and Life in 2030: One Hundred Year Study on Artificial Intelligence, Report of the 2015-2016 Study Panel, Stanford University, Stanford, CA, Sep 2016. http://ai100.stanford.edu/2016-report.

Yoshua, B. (2009). Learning Deep Architectures for AI. Foundations and Trends in Machine Learning 2(1): 1-127.

Defense Science Board (DSB) *Summer Study on Autonomy*. U.S. Department of Defense, p. 4, June 2016.

Endsley, Mica R., *From Here to Autonomy: Lessons Learned from Human-Automation Research.* SA Technologies, Mesa, AZ. December 2016.
Benefits and Risks of Artificial Intelligence, https://futureoflife.org/background/benefits-risks-of-artificial-intelligence/?cn-reloaded=1&cn-reloaded=1

National Science and Technology Committee (NSTC) Networking and Information Technology Research and Development (NITRD) Subcommittee *The National Artificial Intelligence Research and Development Strategic Plan*. Executive Office of the President of the United States, Washington DC, October 2016.

Systems Engineering Transformation and Culture Change

Anne O'Neil, Systems Catalyst and Strategist, Anne O'Neil Consultants, LLC

Systems Engineering is a discipline and practice undergoing transformation. As with other engineering fields, digital tools are enabling the discipline to transition from formerly, primarily paper-based practice. This poses changes to its practitioners as well as to the organizations in which and for which Systems Engineering (SE) practitioners perform their systems activities and generate outcomes and/or deliverables. Equally, Systems Engineering practices are currently being introduced and adapted to a wide range of application domains, particularly infrastructure sectors, where Systems Engineering is not already explicit and where traditional business practices can pose a challenging if not hostile native environment. Whereas SE has traditionally been applied to defense, aerospace and aviation, the domains non-native to SE-application will be referred to as 'non-traditional SE domains'.

INCOSE's SE Vision 2025 predicted, "Systems Engineering will grow and thrive because it brings a multi-disciplinary perspective that is critical to systems product innovation, defect reduction and customer satisfaction. Systems Engineering will be recognized broadly by governments and industry as a discipline of high value to a wide spectrum of application domains because the above contributions, combined with assessment and management of risk and complexity, are key to competitiveness in many industries" (INCOSE 2014). The reality to date, based on over a decade of collaboration with and guidance to systems advocates in 'non-traditional SE domains', suggests these systems advocates struggle for their organizations to experience SE practices as consistently offering 'high value'. This commentary will look at the change dynamics surrounding SE application to non-traditional SE domains as an analog for the cultural change Model-based Systems Engineering (MBSE) poses to traditional SE

[117]

cultures; outlining where SE practices represent transformative change to industry culture and suggesting change strategies for consideration.

Infrastructure domains, ranging from automotive and ground transportation sectors to smart building, biomedical/healthcare, energy, water, and telecom, are experiencing unparalleled levels of complexity and integration as they have increasingly leveraged technology-based solutions to achieve more operationally efficient and customer-focused amenities. These historically civil-structural fields are now deploying communication networks and software intensive systems. Characteristic attributes of these non-traditional SE domains do not naturally favor systems practices, as outlined by the following contrasts.

Siloed operating. These domains feature a history of siloed-working within organizations. Technical disciplines are segregated, as are operational functions from engineering functions, and project teams are usually segregated by physical asset classes.

Shifting interfaces. Typically, interactions between organizational functions are lightly coordinated. The nature of interfaces has historically been minimal in number, loosely-coupled and predominantly physical – civil-structural or architectural type interfaces that could be seen and touched. Whereas today, with the prevalence of software and communication-networks, interfaces have become orders-of-magnitude greater in number and are functional or logical, no longer physical.

"Bottom up" building blocks to "top-down" definition of integrated functionality. Design re-use is predicated on aggregating equipment or component level "building blocks" into functional outcomes. However, technology enables an ever-expanding array of integration options and integrated performance outcomes, which makes desired integrated outcomes exceedingly difficult if not impossible to deliver, if the Owner has not thoroughly described the intended integrated operational performance and functionality from the outset. With bottom-up design approaches, these domains have no concept phase activities that explore intended operational outcomes.

Dominant knowledge not aligned to risk. Given current levels of technology deployment, the risk to project delivery and integration risk no longer resides in the historically core civil-structural (or electro-mechanical) disciplines; it is found in software, digital technologies and communication networks. Yet most infrastructure programs still focus on the large dollars associated with heavy civil construction; as the primary risk no longer resides within the traditional knowledge-base of program managers and industry leaders.

To make a compelling case for changing business practices, requires a sufficiently compelling business case that the new practices proposed will deliver value. Systems advocates must articulate and demonstrate how SE practices offer value – focusing on the Purpose for performing SE, not on performing SE for its own sake. As Beasley and O'Neil, 2016 point out, "[a] persistent focus on merely performing SE activities and processes as prescribed by any number of SE standard processes (INCOSE, ISO, IEEE, etc.) without any attention or focus on the value delivered by such activities does not strengthen the business case for SE adoption." They additionally to assert that "SE application must be tailored to both the specific needs of the problem AND the existing capability of the organization – focused on finding the 'sweet spot'."

For SE practitioners to insert themselves within organizations with siloed working models and without a legacy of systems thinking, to truly serve as 'integrators', 'synthesizers', and 'connectors' across technical disciplines and operational functions, requires that they bring tools and techniques that enable such interactions and ways of engaging. The language and domain familiarity of these systems practitioners to align their activities to business needs and risks as well as to articulate their business case in terms that decision-makers and project managers find convincing is crucial. "It is difficult to sell something if you do not use language intelligible to your prospective customers." (Elliott, et al 2011).

IFSR Conversation 2018

"Unfamiliar terms and new concepts offered by systems engineering pose a challenge – obviously signaling change, something new and different, which for established industries and organizations with strong institutional culture can garner reactions of distrust, skepticism or outright refusal. It also creates a dynamic that places significant reliance upon organizations' leaders (cultivated Systems Champions) to see (or hear) past the unfamiliar terms to embrace the value proposition. Without available systems translation guides, expansion of the practice is heavily dependent upon Systems Advocates." (Beasley and O'Neil, 2016).

To cope with and neutralize the negative reactions to change that new practices engender, there are strategies to consider adopting to support the desired organizational transformation and help sustain changes to culture. Organizational change practices should always be enlisted as strategic means to guide cultural transformation and support sustained change. The following practices have proved beneficial to the author and peer Systems Advocates as they have introduced systems practices to non-traditional SE domains.

Outcomes-based communication. Executives decision-makers and project managers focus on what they are measured against, performance or delivery outcomes. Are we articulating the purpose for systems implementation or application of SE tools in light of the outcomes they will support or achieve? Are we clear about the purpose our SE activities will serve – and will it demonstrably deliver outcomes?

Delivering value. SE application carries the reputation, deservedly or not, of adding burdensome overhead, more than a reputation of adding value. To ensure SE practices gain credibility and become sought by organizations and project teams, SE practitioners must make SE tailoring and scaling decisions that align to business needs and consistently deliver value. The goal is to create a "pull" from the organization – so SE applications must always err on the side of producing tangible results. Are we tailoring our SE implementation so that we will build credibility and make a consistent business case for adopting SE and strengthening systems practices and expertise?

Incremental implementation. Reinforcing SE value particularly in an environment unexposed and unfamiliar with the practices, is aided when implementation can be made incrementally – and aligned with organizational need. Leverage any existing organizational practices, even the smallest kernels of which can serve to be expanded upon into desired change in practices. It builds on what is familiar to the organization, providing a habitual touch points that will help ease cultural change. As the organization experiences small successes as it adopts new practices, this too will support change and provide tangible experiences for early adopters and skeptics alike to be persuaded. Do we seek and create opportunities for incremental implementation as a means to build confidence and momentum to support and sustain change?

Cultivate Executive Sponsors. When addressing organizational cultural change, we must have executive support to remove systemic barriers and organizational structures that reinforce traditional practices that require change. It is critical to develop, inform and sustain Executive Sponsors that recognize the business value, articulate and propagate the need for change and provide reinforcing actions that support the new business practices. It the organization at-large does not see executive alignment and consistent reinforcement, change will not be sustained. Are we cultivating and sustain Executive Sponsors?

Translating transformation and cultural change in non-traditional SE domains to Model-based Systems Engineering (MBSE). MBSE serves as an enabling SE tool; therefore, it must strive to enable clarity, generate meaningful synthesis and insight, which delivers tangible value. MBSE must ultimately serve the *end-users* of SE deliverables, which are not other SE practitioners but executive decision-makers, project managers and operations managers. Our SE practices and by extension, our SE tools need to illuminate complexity, not add to it. MBSE can ultimately be a powerful tool – visualizations

[119]

fundamentally inform and bring clarity, as the proverbial 'a picture is worth a thousand words' tells us. Effectively defining unexplored interactions and illustrating unrecognized interdependencies can powerfully demonstrate value – if that visual information is depicted in a form accessible to the viewers, whose executive and operational decisions drive appropriate shift in business actions that mitigate understood project delivery risks and re-align design teams to achieve desired operational outcomes. We must continue to strive for MBSE to become clearer and more accessible to those served by the application of SE practice.

The organizational cultural barriers and challenges facing SE practitioners when introducing unfamiliar SE practices to non-traditional SE industries are analogous to SE practitioners developing and applying MBSE into environments new to the enabling digital tool and practice. We would be wise to examine the transformative cultural change required to adopt MBSE – as well as consider the transformative cultural change SE practices require to an increasing number of diversifying "non-traditional" application domains. So we appropriately attend to the dynamics associated with cultural change, ensuring our SE practices and tools add meaningful value and we undertake appropriate strategies to ensure effective and sustained SE adoption, which equates to change in business practices.

References:

Beasley, R., O'Neil, A. (2016) *Selling Systems Engineering by Searching for the Sweet Spot*, INCOSE International Symposium, 26: 300-317. https://doi.org/10.1002/j.2334-5837.2016.00161.x

Elliott, B., O'Neil, A., Roberts, C., Schmid, F. and Shannon, I., 2011, "*Overcoming Barriers to Transferring Systems Engineering Practices into the Rail Sector.*" Syst. Engineering Journal, 15: 203–212. http://dx.doi.org/10.1002/sys.20203

INCOSE, 2014, *A World in Motion: Systems Engineering Vision 2025*; https://www.incose.org/products-and-publications/se-vision-2025.

Friday, April 13, 2018:

Report – A Model-based Manifesto

Similar to the values and principles defined as the Agile Manifesto developed by the Agile Alliance for software development and ideas on how data-driven methods would help to instantiate these principles within programs – can we define an Agile or Model-based Engineering manifesto? We successfully culminated this week-long conversation with four Value Statements and a Model-based Engineering (MBE) Manifesto, made up of seven principles.

We have nailed our manifesto to the front door at the MORS 86th Symposium (June, 2018), Monterey, CA, the INCOSE International Symposium, (July, 2018), Washington D.C., the 36th International Conference of the System Dynamics Society, (August, 2018), Reykjavik, Iceland, and the NDIA 21st Annual Systems Engineering Conference, (October, 2018), Tampa, FL, as well as several smaller and local conferences and venues. Our manifesto is currently posted in the Pentagon, Washington, D.C., as well as at each of our respective organizations.

We sincerely hope that you will give feedback and input to the manifesto. While we recognize that not everyone will share our views or appreciate the nuance of our wording, our hope is that the MBE manifesto will embody our full collective values and principles on where the engineering industry is moving forward into the next decades.

We present our value statement here:

Faced with increasing system complexity, interdependencies, breakdown of document-based methods, and other challenges, MBE provides the transformation in which we value:

- ❶ *Information over artifacts*
- ❷ *Integration over independence*
- ❸ *Expressiveness with rigor over flexibility*
- ❹ *Model usage over model creation*

We value the items on the right, but not at the sacrifice of the items on the left.

Figure 15: MBE Manifesto Value Statements

The first section of our manifesto is about our over-arching values. Note the fine print... *that items on the right are values, but not at the sacrifice of the items on the left.* By this statement, we indicate our agreement that the items on the right of the value statements are valuable. For example, we acknowledge that artifacts will always be with us. Independence in model development enables models to be focused on the problem to be solved. Flexibility in one's approach enables innovation. And this group certainly favors models to be created. However, we feel that the values stated on the left of the statements provide more value and help to drive us to more complete, informative, innovative, and useful models. Our ultimate objective is for models to be used and reused.

Explanation of the Value Statements

By **Chris Schreiber, Senior Manager, Lockheed Martin Space Systems – Systems Engineering Modernization**

Information over **artifacts** –

Conventional engineering practices focus on the generation of artifacts to codify and communicate design information. These artifacts often collect and present that design information relative to specific stakeholder groups and concerns, leading to the same information being reused and repackaged across many artifacts. In a model-based engineering paradigm information can be easily assembled in a variety of forms, for a variety of purposes easily. As a result, the engineering job and our engineering processes must focus less on the generation of those artifacts, but on the information needed to generate any artifact for any stakeholder viewpoint.

Integration over **independence**

Conventional engineering practice relies on decomposition and separation of concerns to produce designs that meet complex challenges. This is typically accomplished by dividing the engineering job by domain or subsystem requiring the disintegrated groups to come together periodically at milestones to reintegrate design information. The model-based engineering approach, on the other hand, allows for design information to remain integrated over a project life cycle. Design information from different model-based domains can be related, allowing the collective, integrated design to be continually consistent.

Expressiveness with rigor over **flexibility**

Contemporary engineering practice relies on flexibility, or freedom to communicate design and design information in ways best fitting the needs of the designer themselves. While an unconstrained designer can easily communicate on their terms the elements of their design, this leaves much of interpretation up to a user of that information. In the model-based engineering paradigm, that information must be consumed, in a variety of ways, without the complication of ambiguity and interpretation. In fact, the model-based engineering requires the linguistic features of semantics and syntax to ensure that interpretation is not ambiguous and unpredictable, while still providing sufficient freedom to completely define design. This, we describe as a duality of rigor and expressiveness, enabling complete and consistent use of modeled engineering design.

Model usage over **model creation**

Very often our engineering approaches and tools focus on the capture of information to completely specify a design. This focus emphasizes capturing, storing and communicating this information from the perspective of the designer themselves, without much regard for consumers of the design information. The model-based engineering paradigm values the use of design information beyond mere creation. An emphasis on usage requires additional attention and effort to be paid to contextualizing and understanding not only the design, but design's intent to fully appreciate and leverage this information across the total enterprise.

Explanation of the Principles

By Edward R. Carroll, Principal Systems R&D Analyst, Sandia National Laboratories

The principles:

On behalf of stakeholders, MBE increases emphasis on describing the nature and content of the information produced and consumed, compared to the traditional emphasis on engineering process and procedure.

This topic sounds like a platitude, but it is our collective experience, validated by published research and analysis that MBE provide visual, textual, contextual, relational, behavioral, and parametric perspectives to the information that defines a systems. In this sense, these multiple perspectives improve the communication with stakeholders, enabling a better grasp on what is being developed for their needs. Multiple perspectives likewise increases the information gathered and developed about the system and directs the focus of engineering on the system, not on how the system is to be developed – processes and procedures.

We recognize that—independent of specific Information format, structure, language, syntax, the sequence or order of its production and consumption, and the domains and environments of our projects—the underlying nature (semantics) of the essential information we seek to discover and produce is invariant because of the very nature of engineering.

We refer in this principle to the underlying semantic ontology inherent in all engineering models. Again, our collective experience is validated by published research and analysis. The essential information contained within an engineering model is in digital form software that can be interpreted by other software programs. The invariant underlying semantic ontology is what enables digital engineering models to be integrated across components, systems, programs, and engineering disciplines.

An essential and dynamically changing property of model information is its credibility to those people and processes which will consume that information. The critical nature of some intended uses of model information sets a higher bar on required investment in model verification, validation and uncertainty quantification.

When system concepts are small and contained, it is easy to understand the credibility of the models for that system. As models grow in complexity, the credibility of the associated models becomes less apparent. In a complex system with hundreds of models, thousands of object descriptions, and millions of information nodes, it become impossible for the model to deemed credible by simple observation. The more critical the system, to operations or even to life, the more important that associated models be credible. Verification, validation, and uncertainty quantification take on an increasingly important role to ensure model credibility. Due to the critical nature of some intended uses, the role of V&V and uncertainty quantification may surpass more traditional system design roles in importance.

Principles of human-machine interaction applied to the targeted stakeholders are vital to success. Application of advanced visualization methods and augmented intelligence capabilities can advance that success.

All systems are developed for human use or human stakeholders in one form or another. Consideration of that human-machine interaction should be the focus of the system development. As stated above, digital models gather and develop greater information and multiple perspectives – that can improve the communication to the human stakeholders, as well as to the human-in-the-loop, human-interacting with the machine, or just human user. As also stated above, digital engineering models are software, therefore software-based augmented intelligence capabilities can, and should, be used to advance the success of the human-machine interaction.

We seek an extended team across engineering disciplines with common and integrated understanding of the identity and nature of the model information as well as its content.

We stated above that our definition of MBE is intended to be inclusive of all engineering model disciplines. This integrated community view, based on our own collective experience, and validated by research and analysis, improves system development, operational use, and sustainment by establishing a common and integrated understanding of the system. No more systems need be developed from truckloads of paper documents that are unsearchable, non-integrated, and uncommunicable.

We seek effective enterprise-wide reuse of model-based information to more fully leverage past individual or local learning.

Useful models, because they are useful, are by nature reused. Model reuse saves time, energy, and promotes model credibility. The advantage of digital models is the ease with which knowledge contained within a model can be shared and distributed. Local, expert, mature, and specialized knowledge can and should be leveraged. Leveraging past individual or local learned knowledge is the basis for improving what, where, when, and how systems are developed.

Systems engineering performed according to the above principles is required for the Engineering System itself, a complex and evolving system.

It needs to be recognized that the engineering system that creates the system to be engineered must be engineered, in itself. Our collective experiences are once again validated by research and analysis that a haphazard approach results in a haphazard system. Successfully developed complex systems require engineering rigor applied in a repeatable, tailorable, measured, and optimal approach.

A Model-Based Engineering (MBE) Manifesto

The result of our week-long Conversation culminated into a manifesto on model-based engineering (see the full manifesto in Figure 3 below). We have received considerable feedback on this manifesto, but the ideals that originated this manifesto have held steady. It is our specific intent to spark broad conversation about these ideals. To that end, you (the reader) may or may not agree with the values and principles stated, but our hope is that you will converse about those issues, even argue about them, either with us or with your own colleagues. It is through that conversation that we believe change will happen (whether positive or not remains to be seen).

Figure 16: MBE Manifesto

From 1998 to 2018 : Fuschl Conversations

1998; Hotel Seewinkel, the original location of the Fuschl/IFSR Conversations (1998)

2018: Janie Chroust: Seminar hotel St. Magdalena, garden

Seminarhotel St. Magdalena, front

Seminarhotel St. Magdalena, garden

View of Linz

IFSR Logo 1981 - 2013

IFSR Logo since 2013

www.ingramcontent.com/pod-product-compliance
Lightning Source LLC
LaVergne TN
LVHW022350060326
832902LV00022B/4350